ETERNAL
VIGILANCE

✵ ✵ ✵ ✵

STEVEN HIGGS

ETERNAL
VIGILANCE

Nine Tales of

Environmental

Heroism in

Indiana

Indiana University Press

Bloomington • Indianapolis

The paper used in this publication meets the minimum requirements of American National Standard for Information Sciences—Permanence of Paper for Printed Library Materials, ANSI Z39.48-1984.

Manufactured in the United States of America

Library of Congress Cataloging-in-Publication Data

Higgs, Steven, date
Eternal vigilance : nine tales of environmental heroism in Indiana
/ Steven Higgs.
      p.   cm.
ISBN 0-253-32895-0 (cl). —ISBN 0-253-20971-4 (pbk.)
1. Environmentalists—Indiana—Biography.
2. Environmentalism—Indiana—History—
20th century. I. Title.
GE198.I6H54 1995
363.7'009772—dc20   94-47616

1 2 3 4 5 — 00 99 98 97 96 95

*As is everything in my life, this book
is dedicated to Jessica and Crystal.*

CONTENTS

Introduction   ix

1   A N D Y   M A H L E R
   Saving the Forests   1

2   S U E   L Y N C H
   Fighting Garbage Men in Suits   21

3   T O M   D U S T I N
   Saving Indiana's Rivers from the Corps of Engineers   43

4   T E R R I   M O O R E
   Stopping Out-of-State Waste   65

5   J E F F   S T A N T
   Organizing the State   91

6   B O B   K L A W I T T E R
   Blocking an $80 Million Theme Park   115

7   J O H N   F O S T E R
   Killing an Incineration Experiment   135

8   J O H N   B L A I R
   Watching the Valley   161

9   H E R B   A N D   C H A R L O T T E   R E A D
   Creating and Protecting a National Park   183

INTRODUCTION

The ten people whose stories I tell in the following pages fit any definition of the term *hero* that I can imagine. My dictionary defines heroes as people with great courage and whose exploits are to be admired. To me, a hero is someone who, against all odds and oftentimes at great expense and/or peril, dedicates him- or herself selflessly to a worthy cause.

The subjects in this book are people from all walks of Hoosier life who fit both of those definitions. Their education levels range from high school graduates to Ph.D.s. They live in every corner of the state. They are farmers and teachers, engineers and housewives, political activists and professionals. All have suffered and sacrificed in defense of the environment. Some have nearly gone bankrupt. Others have lost jobs. Most have been the object of scorn and retribution from those in positions of power.

The one thing they all have in common is an unflagging commitment to protecting and improving and preserving Indiana's environment. Because of them, Indiana is a little bit better place for all of us to live in. As a result of their efforts, sand dunes that are home to thousands of plant and animal species still rise above Lake Michigan; giant tracts of the Hoosier National Forest are off limits to chainsaws; the Wabash River remains the longest unprotected river in America that hasn't been channelized for barge traffic; semi loads of East Coast garbage roar past the Center Point Landfill on their way west without stopping in Indiana; no nuclear power plants exist in Indiana; eagles nest on Tillery Hill; an experimental toxic-waste incinerator doesn't spew dioxins and other deadly chemicals over the city of Bloomington and Indiana University.

If more people listened to the environmentalists in this book and supported their efforts, our air would be cleaner, our water clearer, more of our landscapes natural and beautiful, not developed and poisoned and blighted.

While these ten Hoosier environmental heroes can lay claim to tremendous victories fought on behalf of us all, their accomplishments must be kept in perspective. Any one of these folks would tell you unblinkingly that yes, they have won some important and impressive battles, but they and the people of Indiana have been losing the war for generations.

Indiana's environment is an embarrassment of epic proportions. And the state's efforts at environmental protection are a disgrace.

The pathetic condition of Indiana's environment is as palpable as the filthy air that cloaks northwest Indiana. The evidence is shamefully clear in the latest "Green Index," a state-by-state evaluation of the country's environmental health published by Island Press. According to the 1991-92 index, Indiana ranks 43rd in the nation when 256 indicators of environmental health are compared. State spending on environmental protection and natural resources is 47th. A composite of 179 indicators of "Green Conditions" ranks the state 49th. In water pollution, Indiana ranks 49th; in air pollution, 50th; in toxic, hazardous, and solid wastes, 50th; in fun and life quality, 50th.

The idea for this book grew in part out of those numbers. While brainstorming one morning with my publisher about book ideas, we briefly talked about the Green Index. He mentioned that he would be interested if I wanted to do something on Indiana's environmental heroes. The more I thought about it, the more it seemed obvious that this was the book I had been working toward since I first got into journalism in 1983. I wrote my final master's project at the Indiana University School of Journalism in 1985 on clearcutting in the Hoosier National Forest. From there I got on at the Bloomington *Herald-Telephone,* now the *Herald-Times,* where I have covered environmental affairs continuously since 1985.

My plan for this first book was to simply let these amazing people tell their stories their way. And that is pretty much what I have done, though I have tapped other sources for details and perspective. These are the stories of particular environmental struggles as seen through the eyes and visions of those who carry the Earth's flag. No doubt, representatives from Waste Management, the timber industry, Public Service Indiana, the mayor of Bloomington, and other enemies of the environmental heroes written about here would likely tell entirely different versions of these tales. To borrow from Vonnegut, so it goes.

By sharing these stories, I hope to achieve a couple of goals. First and foremost is to recognize and celebrate the selfless actions and superhuman commitments made by each of these ten environmental warriors. Every Hoosier's hat should be off to them. I also hope to provide a picture of the environmental movement itself, its strengths and weaknesses, the basic tenets of its philosophy. Finally, it's my hope that the profiles in courage told here will inspire others to follow their leads. To aid in that quest, each of the ten discusses the strategies he or she pursued and offers advice to the next generation of Hoosier environmental heroes.

The title *Eternal Vigilance* comes from conversations I have had with leading environmentalists in the course of my eleven years writing about the Indiana environment. It is a theme that inevitably comes up in any extended discussion with a seasoned enviro in Indiana, or anywhere else, for that matter. Battles are won, but more are lost. And the war never ends. Just before Jeff St. Clair left Indiana for the Pacific Northwest, he and I sat down on the porch of his Brown County cabin and talked about the then-fresh victory in the Hoosier National Forest land-management plan. He put the dilemma in perspective by deferring to the observations of David Brower. When industry wins an environmental skirmish, it wins for good. When environmentalists win, they achieve stays of execution.

Altogether, the environmentalists profiled here have devoted roughly 164 years to the fight, only to see their state's environment and quality of life ravaged day in and day out by business and industry, with acquiescence from their rubber stamps in the Indiana legislature and an apathetic public. As these words are being written in the spring of 1994, state officials in Indianapolis are quaking in their boots at the possibility that national environmental groups may make Indiana an example of how ineptly environmental protection can be handled. Quake they should, for they would be easy targets.

Without question, many of these stories are not-in-my-backyard reactions to environmental horrors. Sue Lynch, Terri Moore, and Andy Mahler literally reacted to plans that others had for properties adjoining their back yards. For Bob Klawitter, John Foster, Tom Dustin, Jeff Stant, John Blair, and Herb and Charlotte Read, the horrors were developing just beyond their back yards. When the acronym NIMBY is used to describe environmental initiatives, it inevitably is used pejoratively. But should environmental activists apologize when they are accused of NIMBYism? Is there anything more American than fighting to protect one's own back yard? The notion of enlightened self-interest is at the root of American political thought. And there is no more sacred interest within that system than one's property, one's own back yard. For better or worse, that's how it works.

Historically, environmentalists tend to be of two distinct but often overlapping types—activist/humanitarians and scientist/adventurers. Most of the people here have their roots in activist/humanitarian soil, though some have scientific credentials and no doubt have engaged in their share of adventurism.

The predominance of males came about inadvertently. As originally planned, the balance would have been seven men and five women. But as the project progressed, the stories of two of the women didn't fit the overall themes that emerged. One chapter was to be on state senator Vi Simpson and her efforts at legislating on behalf of the environment. But the story of a politician just didn't fit alongside those of grassroots activists. The other was to be on Amy Roche, a young Bloomington environmental activist and a founder of the Student Environmental Action Coalition on the IU campus. I had wanted to include her as an example of the future of Hoosier environmentalism. But Amy has been working on environmental issues for only a few years, while everyone else in the book has been at it for decades. My guess is that if I later decide to revisit the subject of Hoosier environmental heroes, Amy Roche might be one of the profiles.

Over the past year and a half I have had the good fortune to meet and talk with ten of the most extraordinary individuals in the state of Indiana. After listening to them, after getting caught up in their passions and considering the simple truths in their messages, I find it hard to understand why Indiana's environment remains such an embarrassment. Historian James Madison perhaps provided the answer in his book *The Indiana Way: A State History:* "Here as elsewhere many Hoosiers feared that environmental protection meant a loss of individual freedom and a threat to economic growth. Those who believed otherwise often proved insufficiently organized to make their case effectively. The Indiana League of Women Voters was nearly alone in showing serious and sustained attention to environmental issues during the 1970s."

While Madison's last statement is incorrect, as evidenced by the stories told here, his general view seems valid. Despite the efforts of those included in this book, and of the dozens of Indiana environmental leaders not written about here, Hoosiers can't seem to grasp the urgency of the problems. They don't understand the tragedy of being last in environmental protection. They don't see the environment as part of a bigger, critical, ecological and economic whole. Their short-sighted Jacksonian views regarding environmental politics are dangerous and counterproductive. It's like putting sunblock on their noses and leaving the rest of their bodies exposed to the UV rays.

It will take eternal vigilance to turn things around.

ETERNAL
VIGILANCE

ANDY MAHLER

A U.S. Forest Service proposal to build off-road vehicle trails near his land in rural Orange County got Andy Mahler active in environmental politics in 1985. His love of the woods and his experiences fighting the Forest Service have kept him involved and inspired a career that has made him an activist of national stature. Andy helped organize Protect Our Woods to fight the ORV proposal, became a leader in the struggle for the forest, and played a key role in securing one of the state environmental movement's most impressive victories ever. Working in conjunction with activists in southern Indiana and across the state, Andy organized opposition to the Hoosier National Forest Land Management Plan and turned it from one of the worst proposed in the country to one of the best. He now heads Heartwood, a forest-preservation group that has as its goal ending logging in the national forests of the central hardwood region. Andy, forty-four, lives with his wife, Linda Lee, on a farm called the Lazy Black Bear just south of Paoli on the fringes of the Hoosier. He takes care of the farm and works full-time with Heartwood.

ANDY MAHLER

Saving the Forests

1

🌱 🌱 🌱 🌱

Trees have always played an important role in Andy Mahler's life. As a youth growing up in Bloomington, Andy enjoyed playing in the woods, climbing trees, lying on the forest floor gazing upward, losing himself in the serenity of the forest canopy. As a restless nineteen-year-old hitchhiking through southern Indiana, he fell in love with the wooded hills of Orange County. When it came time to settle down eight years later, he returned to those pristine woodlands just south of Paoli, eventually settling in with his future wife, Linda Lee, in a lodge on the farm they call the Lazy Black Bear, a 240-acre plot surrounded by the hardwood trees of the Hoosier National Forest. Together, Andy and Linda spent countless hours hiking and riding their horses along the many trails that lace their forested refuge and the surrounding national forest.

Andy was forty-one when we sat on the porch of the Lazy Black Bear and talked about his career as an environmentalist. The call of the woods still directed his life like an invisible hand. Since 1985, the consuming passion of his life has been saving the woodlands from the designs of those seeking profit from their destruction. In 1985 Andy was one of the founders of Protect Our Woods, a broad-based coalition of Orange County residents who organized to oppose a U.S. Forest Service plan to build 112 miles of off-road-vehicle trails in the Hoosier. Half of those trails would have been in

Orange County. With Andy in one of the primary leadership roles, the group was instrumental not only in defeating the ORV proposal, but in transforming the federal agency's long-term forest-management plan from one of the most resource-exploitative in the country into one of the most environmentally sensitive. Today Andy heads Heartwood, an organization whose name is a blending of heartland and hardwood. Heartwood is a coalition of activists from an eight-state area dedicated to eliminating logging on public lands in the central hardwood region, an area bounded roughly by Pennsylvania, Georgia, Arkansas, and Minnesota.

The Lazy Black Bear is situated at the dead end of a mile-long gravel road that angles off a county road a couple of miles from the nearest highway. Their land is littered with barns and ponds and sheds and stables and gardens, the stuff idyllic country life is made of. The air is filled with the sights and sounds of a veritable menagerie of dogs, cats, horses, geese, ducks, and other critters wild and domestic, along with a never-ending flow of human visitors, which Andy likewise describes as both wild and domestic. Inside the multilevel cabin, nearly every square inch is filled with objets d'art suggestive of comfortable, back-to-the-earth sixties types entering middle age—hand-loomed rugs, graceful antiques, valuable quilts, tasteful furniture, enough odds and ends to keep the curious occupied for days. Photo collages filled with the images of what Linda calls "our celebrity friends"—musicians, writers, political activists—grace the kitchen walls. Indeed, Andy comes from celebrity stock. He is a descendant of the Bohemian-born, romantic-era composer Gustav Mahler.

Andy is tall and lean with chiseled features, black hair highlighted with silver-gray streaks that he wears swept up and back, and glowing blue-gray eyes that emanate intelligence and sensitivity. His movie-star good looks, abundantly apparent in a photo on a shelf at the Lazy Black Bear, once prompted a woman visitor to turn to those of us in the room and observe rhetorically, "Is Andy Mahler a handsome man, or what?" His easy-going, soft-spoken style invites trust, if not affection. People who know Andy Mahler tend to speak fondly of him, regardless of their political or philosophical bent. *Inspirational* and *charismatic* are adjectives commonly used by friends to describe him.

Andy's not certain exactly when the seeds of his destiny as a forest preservationist were sown. It may have been when, as a child, he first experienced the loss of a tree as a personal trauma. One afternoon when he and his mother went to downtown

Bloomington on a shopping trip, they found their beloved tree-lined Kirkwood Avenue nearly stripped of all its trees. In the name of progress, city officials had cut down the trees that formerly had shaded the city's friendliest avenue to make way for parking.

"We were totally unprepared for it," Andy says while sitting in a rocker on his expansive porch, stroking the whiskers of a gray tabby cat that gnaws on his knuckles. They had cut down all the trees starting at the east end of the street, and there were only a handful left standing by the Book Corner. And they fell the next day. "I don't know if that's what set me on the course of wanting to protect trees, but I've always loved trees," Andy now reflects.

Whether or not that experience helped create a mindset that would lead to later passion, there is no doubt what specific events in 1985 sent Andy on a one-way journey down the path of environmental activism.

One of his and Linda's favorite pastimes at the Lazy Black Bear had always been riding their horses on their land and through the Hoosier. While riding one day in 1985, they came across an unsettling scene, a vision that to this day remains etched indelibly upon their minds. Andy describes it: "They had put a couple of clearcuts right in the middle of the only Forest Service–designated horse trail in this area. They didn't even have enough sense to avoid it when they put in a clearcut. It was a scene of utter devastation."

The scene that Andy and Linda rode upon that day was similar to many others that were scattered all over the Hoosier, a 190,000-acre patchwork of hardwood forest that stretches from Monroe and Brown counties on the north through nine southern Indiana counties to the Ohio River. Like their counterparts elsewhere in the country, Forest Service officials at the Hoosier supervisor's office in Bedford had come to rely on clearcutting as their primary land-management tool. The agency and the forest had arrived at this sorry juncture after a tortuous 150-year history.

When the settlers arrived in Indiana in the early 1800s, the rugged hill country that today is occupied by the Hoosier was, like 87 percent of the state, virgin timber—ash, sycamore, elm, walnut, butternut, poplar, cherry, sassafras, persimmon, some seventy species in all. Only a handful of rocky outcrops covered with grassy fields in the forest's southern region were open. While it is unclear exactly which Native American tribes inhabited the knobby hill country and used it for hunting grounds, Delawares, Miamis, Shawnees, Piankeshaws, Wyandottes, and Potawatomies are mentioned in county histories from the Hoosier Forest region.

As hordes of white settlers in search of land migrated down the Ohio from the mid-Atlantic states and overland from the southeast through Tennessee and Kentucky, many headed north from staging towns such as Madison and New Albany into the wilderness that was the Indiana Territory. Settlers, primarily from Kentucky, Tennessee, North Carolina, and Virginia, slowly scratched their way north throughout the mid- and late nineteenth century. They hunted and trapped the astoundingly bountiful game—bear, deer, wild turkey, squirrel, raccoon, passenger pigeon. They cleared the flat ridgetops and stream valleys, mostly to grow corn and raise hogs.

What they found on the land that would become the Hoosier, however, was that most of the soil was suited for growing trees, not crops. As the century progressed, the pioneers found themselves in a never-ending cycle of having to clear more land for crops and animals because previous plots eroded and their soil became depleted. Along the way, they increasingly turned to the land's omnipresent economic asset—its trees—for economic sustenance. In the decade before the turn of the century, Indiana was leading the nation in timber production. By that same time, the once abundant bear, deer, and wild turkey had all disappeared. In 1914, the last passenger pigeon died in captivity.

When the Depression hit in the 1930s, the land that would become the Hoosier was devastated. Ridgetops and valleys, even the hillsides, were denuded of trees. In his 1931 "Game Survey of the North Central States," Aldo Leopold estimated that between 1910 and 1925, eighteen southern Indiana counties had lost a total of 405,000 acres in farmland to erosion and soil depletion. With their lands unsuitable for agriculture and devoid of salable timber, the people were destitute and couldn't pay their bills, or their taxes. Counties took their essentially worthless lands at tax sales.

As President Franklin Roosevelt's New Deal moved to restore economic health to the nation, south-central Indiana was among the areas targeted for relief. The counties, desperate to unload land that was contributing nothing to either the economy or the tax base, and landowners who had not yet lost their land were anxious to sell to the developing National Forest System. In 1935, the Indiana General Assembly passed enabling legislation to allow the Forest Service to purchase land in Indiana. The law designated four "purchase units," areas in which the agency could buy land, limited to 722,500 acres. The agency began purchasing land for the Benjamin Harrison National Forest, which was formally proclaimed the Hoosier National Forest by the secretary of agriculture in 1951.

The Forest Service was created to manage "working forests" for timber production, regulation of navigable streams, and fire protection. Its goal was twofold: to protect natural resources and to enhance local economies. To that end, agency officials utilized workers from Roosevelt's Civilian Conservation Corps and set about reclaiming the land. CCC crews first planted trees on thousands of acres of former farmland to slow erosion. The CCC men worked out of camps operated by the U.S. Army, laboring for the Forest Service and the Indiana Department of Conservation. In addition to replanting the barren landscape, they fought fires, put in telephone lines, and built roads. They constructed the Hickory Ridge Fire Tower, which still stands on the fringe of the Charles Deam Wilderness Area in southeastern Monroe County.

About the only active management activities the agency engaged in for the first thirty years or so involved working cooperatively with state conservation officials to reintroduce game to the forest. In the 1930s they began reintroducing the white-tailed deer, in the 1950s the wild turkey. Land managers produced habitat for these species by creating small openings and wildlife ponds throughout the forest. Other than that, forest management essentially consisted of letting the trees mature.

While the Forest Service claims to have been developing a multiple-use approach to National Forest System management prior to 1960, passage of the Multiple Use–Sustained Yield Act of 1960 by Congress institutionalized the concept and made the agency legally liable for not following that prescription.

The multiple-use doctrine and rapid growth in the popularity of off-road vehicles in the 1960s set the stage for the first showdown between Hoosier environmentalists and the Forest Service. In 1964, a 100-mile ORV race through the forest, called the "Buffalo 100," was held near Brownstown in Jackson County by off-road enthusiasts, with Forest Service knowledge. Agency officials saw ORVs as one of many legitimate uses the public wanted to allow in its national forests. A second such event was held in 1970, this time without agency knowledge, and at a time when concern about ORV damage to forests was growing. A year later the Forest Service banned ORVs from the forest until an ORV management policy could be developed. In 1974, the agency released a plan to develop two sets of ORV trails in the forest, one on the north end and the other on the south, with sixty-six miles of trails traversing 21,464 acres of national forest. The Indiana Division of the Izaak Walton League responded with a lawsuit in federal court. In 1977, a federal judge issued an order banning ORVs from the forest until the Forest Service had completed a land-management plan as required by the National Forest Management Act of 1976. ORV trail plans thus were stymied until 1985, when the agency issued its land-management plan and Andy Mahler got involved in the third major war for the future of the Hoosier National Forest.

The second major war over the Hoosier was sparked in 1973 when the Forest Service began its Roadless Area Review and Evaluation (RARE) program to identify sections in eastern national forests suitable for inclusion in the National Wilderness System. The agency recommended that 15,000 acres of the Hoosier be designated wilderness. The Indiana University–based Indiana Public Interest Research Group (InPIRG) responded with a proposal to expand the wilderness to 32,000 acres, calling it the Nebo Ridge Wilderness Study Area.

The controversy generated by the InPIRG proposal led to the Hoosier wilderness being deleted from the Eastern Wilderness Act of 1975, a second roadless area review by the Forest Service called RARE II, and nine years of exhaustive debate before the Charles Deam Wilderness Area was created in 1982.

The final war for the Hoosier began in January 1984, when the Forest Service released the long-awaited draft of its Hoosier National Forest Land Management Plan. Among its most controversial elements were allowances for oil and gas leasing and off-road vehicle trails, both of which had been on hold for years awaiting the plan.

"Those things now have the potential to re-emerge," Forest Service spokesman Gary Lidholm said at the time the draft was released. "We could be hearing from an awful lot of people."

⁕ ⁕ ⁕ ⁕

The Forest Service did hear from an awful lot of people during the public comment period on the draft plan, and then on the final plan that was adopted on October 17, 1985, thirty days after it had been issued. Coalitions of environmentalists, including veteran forest-issue groups such as the Sassafras Audubon Society from Bloomington and the Izaak Walton League, were joined in the fight by newly formed groups such as ForestWatch. Formed in the summer of 1985, ForestWatch was headed by Jeff St. Clair, who became an instrumental force in the process.

The plan itself not only was the first completed in the Forest Service's eastern region, it also was one of the worst in the country, at least from the perspective of the environmental community. It opened up 81 percent of the forest for timber harvesting over a 120-year period, with clearcutting on plots of up to thirty acres the dominant method. It opened up 90 percent of the forest for oil and gas exploration, even though there was little possibility that oil and gas existed in any but a tiny portion of the forest. It called for 112 miles of ORV trails. It called for timber harvesting on nearly every acre of pristine or ecologically unique areas that environmentalists coveted.

St. Clair succinctly made the environmentalists' case during a November 1985 debate with Forest Service officials in Bloomington: "There's been too much timbering and not nearly as much emphasis on other aspects of the national forest. . . . The Hoosier should provide the high-quality recreational experiences that are growing in demand much faster than the demand for timber." In January 1986, the plan was formally appealed by Sassafras Audubon, the Izaak Walton League, the Hoosier Chapter Sierra Club, ForestWatch, the Indiana University Environmental Law Society, the Indiana and Bloomington chapters of the League of Women Voters, the Monroe County Humane Society, and seventeen individuals.

Hoosier Forest supervisor Harold Godlevske and other agency planners and officials vehemently defended the plan. They argued that clearcutting was an effective timber-harvesting method that not only encouraged regeneration of oak-hickory forests but also provided prime habitat for game animals, which need forest edge for food. Logging roads provided recreation, as hikers, hunters, and others used them for trails. And ORVs simply were considered as legitimate a use of forest resources as any other. In short, the plan was intended to provide multiple-use benefits to a variety of forest users. "There are a lot of different publics that we're dealing with and trying to be responsive to," Godlevske said in January 1986. "It puts us in a position of trying to balance opposing viewpoints on how the forest should be managed."

Environmentalists had always seen such arguments as nothing more than hollow rationalizations for continued overharvesting. The Forest Service, after all, was populated mostly by foresters, and foresters see trees as commodities to be cut. Jeff St. Clair in July 1985: "The Forest Service's policy has been to use every compartment of the Hoosier National Forest for all purposes. The overuse of each compartment is demeaning the entire national forest and wiping out the value for most uses. ForestWatch will actively monitor the Forest Service to make sure the national forest is managed in a way that is consistent with the various needs of the public and not solely the demands of the timber industry."

When Andy and Linda rode onto the clearcut near their land, the final Hoosier National Forest Land Management Plan had not yet been released. When he and Linda first saw the clearcut, Andy didn't know much about clearcutting. In fact, he wasn't even sure that the denuded land he had ridden upon was National Forest land. He later learned that it was. He also heard about the November 1985 debate in Bloomington. He and Linda attended, and they were appalled by what they heard from the Forest Service. "They seemed real imperious," Andy says. "You know, 'We are the experts, we know what's right. If only the public had more information, they'd understand why we do what we do, and they'd fall in line behind our leadership.'"

While Andy found the clearcut offensive and the Forest Service's attitude arrogant and insulting, he wasn't quite ready to take up the fight. That readiness didn't develop until September, when he and Linda received a notice in the mail from the Forest Service outlining the plans for the ORV trails. As part of the management plan, Forest Service officials planned to build fifty-five miles of trail in a part of Orange County called Little Africa. The site of a nineteenth-century black settlement, the area was rich in cultural history. The idea of whining, mud-slinging motorcycles gouging ruts across Little Africa just seemed obscene to the Mahlers.

They knew a little bit about ORVs from personal experience. Once a year, a group of ORV enthusiasts held an event they called the "Chicken Mud Run" through the Hoosier near Andy's and Linda's land. About a hundred four-wheelers would camp out in the forest and buzz the hills. "They would just tear the heck out of it," Andy says. "They preferred wet weather, and they preferred mud. They preferred hills; they wanted a challenge, going places they had no business going. They tore down a neighbor's fence and did doughnuts in a nearby cornfield. We knew we sure didn't want them in the forest."

Andy and Linda learned from some neighbors that an informational meeting was scheduled in Paoli, and they decided to attend. Even though the town was drenched in a torrential rain that November evening, about fifty people jammed into a room at the county courthouse annex. Those attending learned that there was more to the forest-management plan they had only recently heard of than just ORVs and a few clearcuts. They learned about the oil and gas leasing. They learned that the plan, with the exception of the ORV proposal, was already in effect. In a strategic move, Forest Service officials had separated the ORV proposal from the rest of the plan. They realized it would be a nasty, difficult fight to win, and they did not want it to hinder progress on the overall management plan.

Andy and Linda also discovered that many of their friends and neighbors in Orange County shared their outrage at what was happening with regard to the forest. "At the time it was all totally alien to us," Andy says. "We didn't know what oil and gas leasing on the forest would entail. We knew what ORVs sounded like. We knew what a clearcut looked like. I guess that was our starting point."

Also attending were some environmentalists from Bloomington who had been fighting the management plan. Veteran Forest Service fighter Bill Hayden said that the forest battle entered a new phase that night. "Basically, I told them they could beat it, but nobody could beat it for them. They had to do it," Hayden says.

And that's just what happened. After that meeting, a group of Orange County residents decided that they needed to form a group to oppose the Forest Service. "You only notice a group like the Forest Service when they do something you disapprove of," Andy says. "If they're doing things that are reasonable, nobody's going to complain. But the clearcuts and the ORV trails seemed unreasonable to the vast majority of citizens in Orange County, or at least that's what we believed. And we set out to prove it."

The first thing the group did was hold a meeting, at which the name "Protect Our Woods" was chosen because of its aggressive title and the strong statement created by its acronym, POW. The original group of about twenty people who attended the first meeting was soon pared down to twelve or thirteen. Because Andy had the most free time of any of them—"I was the unemployed member of our twosome," he says of himself and Linda, a schoolteacher—he was elected president.

POW members decided to focus their efforts on two primary objectives. First, they wanted to change the focus of Forest Service timber harvesting from clearcutting to selective cuts. On this point they had support from smaller loggers in the region, who felt that they were being cut out of national forest timber sales because only large operations had the wherewithal to cut thirty-acre plots at a time. Second, they planned to take on the ORV proposal full-force. They were 100 percent opposed to off-road vehicles and decided not to compromise or accept any demonstration projects involving the national forest.

At the time, the goals of Protect Our Woods were short-term. But Andy was looking ahead. "I do remember that I was the principal advocate that, whatever the outcome of the ORV appeal, we would do what we could to get the plan re-evaluated," he says. "I did not feel that Orange County people had had a reasonable opportunity to comment."

Protect Our Woods had no time to waste, as under Forest Service rules the public had only ninety days to comment on the ORV proposal. By the time Andy and POW got organized, there was only a month or so left. They had to educate themselves on the issue and the process and mobilize public support, all between Thanksgiving and Christmas of 1985.

To make progress toward both goals of education and mobilization, POW called a public meeting and invited former Hoosier National Forest supervisor Claude Ferguson to speak. Ferguson had lost his job during the first ORV debate, primarily for filing an affidavit accusing the Forest Service of malfeasance over the ORV issue. Andy and POW publicized the meeting by putting up posters, calling people on the phone, contacting the media, anything they could think of to get the word out.

The meeting was held at the Orange County 4H building on December 5, 1985, and the Forest Service was invited to defend the ORV proposal. About 150 people showed up, and it turned into an emotional shouting match between pro- and anti-ORV forces. Most were landowners opposed to the trail plan. Landowner Allen Seiler summed up the opposition: "I moved here from Milwaukee to get away from the noise, and now they tell me they are going to allow ORVs in the forest. I don't want to be bothered by a bunch of belligerent bikers." Two weeks later, Forest Service officials canceled a planned public forum in Paoli on the ORV plan, citing concern for their safety.

While everyone at the December 5 meeting was overwhelmingly opposed to both clearcutting and ORVs, Andy says that there seemed to be stronger opposition to clearcutting. That helped convince him that his sense that POW should stay after the plan beyond the ORV proposal was on target.

As part of their plan, Andy and other POW folks also got to know their enemy—the Forest Service—from whom they would receive valuable information more than once. For example, though he felt they were doing a good job with the letter-writing campaign, Andy was astonished when agency officials told him that letters were running anywhere from 9 to 1 to 99 to 1 in favor of the ORV plan. He later learned that a deputy supervisor on the Hoosier, in a national ORV magazine, had encouraged ORV enthusiasts to write the agency voicing their support to offset the anticipated opposition from the environmental community.

In light of that information, POW set as its chief objective getting the public comment period extended. To accomplish that goal, they went to work on politicians, mindful of how the political process operates. They didn't try to persuade the politicians to take POW's side; they merely asked them to use their influence to have the public comment period extended. They wanted to get them involved in the issue without forcing them to commit to any particular position. "Politicians don't want to get out front on an issue," Andy says. "With few exceptions, they are not really leaders. They consider it their responsibility to see which way the wind is blowing and then get out front and wave the flag after it's already clear which way the army's marching. They didn't know how it would come out. So we just asked them for something reasonable."

Among those who wrote letters were the county commissioners, a local judge, the Paoli town board, the county surveyor, the soil and water conservation board, and the Paoli Garden Club. POW ultimately succeeded in getting the comment period extended another ninety days. And ORV opponents used that time to their advantage.

At one point they decided that since the letters were running 9 to 1 or even 99 to 1 against them, they should go to the Forest Service and read the letters. By so doing, they learned more about how the Forest Service was working against them. They learned that agency officials had counted an anti-ORV petition with twelve hundred signatures as one response. But forty identical form letters supporting the trails were counted as one each.

They also found additional arguments for their positions in letters opposing the ORV proposal. And they obtained names for the POW mailing list, which became the basis of their political power. Using that power base to full advantage, POW started publishing a monthly newsletter, polling people, working on politicians, getting its message out. The end result was that the anti-ORV forces began to catch up with their opposition toward the end of the first ninety-day public comment period, though they were still behind when it ended. The Forest Service ultimately received more than seventeen hundred letters on the ORV proposal. And by the end, it was clear where public sentiment lay. "In the second three months, we totally blew them away," Andy says. "That extension made an enormous difference."

Winning the letters battle, however, was not tantamount to winning the war. Forest Service officials remained committed to both their ORV proposal and the Hoosier management plan, despite clear signs of growing public opposition. But along the way, Andy learned some important bits of information from regional forester Larry Henson, information that he and POW would exploit. Henson told Andy that the Hoosier at that time was the second smallest national forest in the country, that it had the second more fragmented land-ownership pattern of any national forest, and that the Hoosier ORV proposal had generated the most controversy *anywhere*. From that point forward, Protect Our Woods made those themes central to its arguments against the ORV proposal, citing them again and again in public meetings, to the press, and in letters to the editors of local newspapers.

In June 1986, the Forest Service, sensing that public opposition to the plan was overwhelming them, set up a negotiation session with a professional mediator to work out a compromise between the two sides. Pro- and anti-ORV representatives met in Bloomington on June 24 to hash it out. Andy told the press: "We are prepared to proceed with conciliation and negotiation because we think it is a valuable and useful process, but only on the condition that the conciliation and negotiation pursue options outside the Hoosier National Forest. If that's an option that's viable, then we're prepared to pursue this as long as it takes." But, he said, the responsibility for deciding the issue rested with the Forest Service, not the warring parties. "We didn't really want to shut off discussion, but we wanted to make our opposition to ORVs in the Hoosier National Forest quite plain and unambiguous. We wanted to not make our 'no' the final say. . . . We wanted to put the issue where it belongs, and that's in the hands of the Forest Service, who has to make the decision." The session ended within minutes of its start when ORV proponents walked out.

By year's end it was clear even to the Forest Service what the decision had to be. On December 19, 1986, Godlevske announced that he was recommending that the trails not be built. "We made the best attempt we could to accommodate ORV use and determined that it still conflicted with local landowners," he said at the time. "The realities of the situation are that the forest has thousands of neighbors out there, and it is important that we are considerate of their needs and concerns."

On the following April 3, regional forester Floyd "Butch" Marita, who had replaced Henson as head of Region 9, announced that the ORV proposal had been withdrawn. Among the reasons Marita cited for the decision were the forest's land-ownership pattern and its small size. He said the agency couldn't guarantee that ORVs wouldn't have a negative impact on private lands, and that the forest was so small that any trails would necessarily result in an excessive impact on the environment. "I believe that most of the concern over the adverse effects of ORV use is founded more on opinion than on facts," Marita said. "There's a large segment of the public that thinks ORV use is harmful to just about everything. This is not true, but I believe my decision, while not ending the controversy, will at least allow some of the old wounds to heal."

Within a very short period of time, the entire Hoosier management plan would suffer the same fate. On June 26, 1987, Marita announced that the environmentalists' position had prevailed. "The plan needs to be revised. We need to make significant changes," he said that day, calling the plan "seriously flawed." The agency later established a "working group" of interested individuals with varying positions to develop a series of alternatives from which the agency would later choose. Among the groups involved were timber industry groups, environmentalists, and Protect Our Woods.

Andy and POW played a significant role in those negotiations, with their position shifted to reflect research by Bob Klawitter, one of the group's other leaders. By early 1987, Klawitter had obtained initial data from a report that the Indiana Department of Natural Resources was preparing on the state's timber inventory. It showed that 88 percent of the state's forests were privately owned, mostly by noncommercial landowners; that the amount of forest land in the state had grown by 10 percent since the last inventory in 1967; and that the forest land base was growing 50 percent faster than it was being cut.

POW at that point, after some soul-searching, altered its position from one of eliminating clearcutting and reducing the amount of timber harvested on the Hoosier to one advocating that no timber be cut at all. The decision was difficult because much of the group's early support had come from small loggers. But knowing that the Forest Service sold its timber at a loss, Andy and POW felt that economic arguments against timber harvesting should prevail. The Forest Service was subsidizing its timber sales with tax dollars and selling the logs in direct competition with private landowners.

When the final Hoosier plan was released in 1990, among the proposals was the "no-cut alternative" put forward by Protect Our Woods. The Forest Service did not adopt that plan, but it did select an alternative written and promoted by the Hoosier Environmental Council that dramatically reduced the amount of timber to be cut, nearly eliminated clearcutting in the forest, protected large segments of environmentally sensitive areas, and was hailed by environmentalists nationwide as one of the best forest-management plans in the country.

HEC had mounted a public campaign on behalf of its position that resulted in 125,000 signatures on petitions supporting the "Conservationist Alternative." And while HEC is largely credited with turning the forest plan around, no one disputes that without the efforts of Andy Mahler and Protect Our Woods, the final plan would have been far different. Just before the formation of Protect Our Woods, some leading environmentalists were concerned that the best they could hope to achieve was protection of some important natural areas in Monroe and Brown counties.

Andy cites three strategies adopted by Protect Our Woods that he believes were key to its success: having local people involved in visible positions within the organization, developing good working relations with the press, and building support with the public and the politicians. The latter two, he argues, follow from the first. "We weren't subject to the charges that we were outsiders butting in and telling people what to do. It was local people taking the lead, and in some very highly visible positions. . . . It's a lot harder to wage a campaign to protect something if it's based somewhere else. Especially if it's an urban-based effort to protect some rural area, you leave yourself wide open to just a handful of local people trying to exploit the resource for profit being able to portray themselves as the locals."

🌽 🌽 🌽 🌽

Andy left Protect Our Woods in 1991, after having formed Heartwood in the fall of 1990, and broadened his arena to the central hardwood region. He took with him the lessons he learned in the Hoosier fight and applied them in Heartwood's efforts to save the central hardwoods.

Heartwood serves as a resource center for groups fighting local forest issues throughout the region. "When it comes to vision, we are the leaders," Andy says. "But that's not where the front line is. The front line is in every single timber sale and oil and gas lease in the region. We are there as the supporter, the resource. We can provide people on the front lines with information and tools and specialists they need to deal with whatever situation they are dealing with."

Fellow Heartwood activist and friend Alison Cochran, however, says Andy's vision is the soul of the Heartwood organization. "We all have responsibility for bringing it together," she says. "But there's no doubt that his leadership has been the consolidating force." That leadership revolves around an intelligence and style that can only be described as inspirational, she says. She calls it Lincolnesque. He has a commanding presence and a great sense of humor. He is polite and respectful of others and humble in the way he presents himself. His intensity and stamina are awe-inspiring. He gets up at dawn to feed the animals on the Lazy Black Bear and then works all day and night—sometimes past midnight—on Heartwood issues. "He's an inspiration," Alison says. "There's so much material that goes through that office, and has for years. And yet each little detail has such a quality about it. He wants it to be the best it can be."

Perhaps Andy's greatest strengths surface when he interacts with others, be they friends or enemies. Regardless of whether he's talking to an adversary, a congressional committee, or a fellow activist, Andy Mahler is pretty much the same guy. "He just talks to them," Cochran says. "He tells them exactly the same thing. It doesn't change one iota from what he would say to you or me."

His approach to organizing allies involves recognizing each person's individual strengths and cultivating them. "He lets people do what they're strongest at and really continues to affirm them," she says. "He helps them be what they will be."

Tom Zeller, a veteran Hoosier Forest fighter from the pre-Protect Our Woods days, says that Andy Mahler and Bob Klawitter are both giants at analyzing public policy and then making arguments that anyone can understand. "They do it by talking sense to people who are used to talking sense," he says. "They talk about the value of woodlots, and of the Forest Service selling timber below what it costs them, and that that's going to lower the value of private woodlots. They don't dramatize situations most of the time. They just sort of analyze it and then tell you in simple terms what's going on."

How much longer and farther Andy will carry his fight to save the forests remains to be seen. Fighting for forest preservation was not something he had ever considered before riding upon that clearcut in 1985. "During the first five years I figured I'd eventually get back to the original conditions of my life," he says. "But I guess I came to realize that there wasn't much that I could be doing with my life that was more important than this as long as we could afford it. Especially once we started winning on the Hoosier, the notion sort of lodged in my mind that you start out doing environmental work to stop something that's wrong, something clearly wrong that's been proposed or implemented—an incinerator, a landfill, a clearcut—and you marshal support against that. But then you recognize that not only is that thing wrong but there is something else that is right. And you sort of have an obligation to at least make an effort or commitment to work toward what's right."

What Andy came to believe is right is bringing an end to logging in the small national forests of the Midwest, specifically the Hoosier, the Wayne in Ohio, the Shawnee in Illinois, the Daniel Boone in Kentucky, and the Mark Twain in Missouri. "I sort of have those as my personal objectives," he says. "And it may not happen. I may stay with this the rest of my life and that not happen. I may leave it in two years and it not happen. Or I may stay with it another five years and get all those things implemented. It's hard to say. I haven't a clue."

Through his efforts, first with Protect Our Woods and then with Heartwood, Andy has become a leader of national stature on forest issues. He regularly testifies before congressional committees on Forest Service funding and other forest issues. In a December 26, 1993, article in the *New York Times* about the split within the Sierra Club over logging policies, Andy was among those whose opinions were included. Identified as "a club member from Paoli, Ind.," he told the paper that if the Sierra Club would take a more combative approach, its membership and revenues would increase. "What we're seeing is how an environmental organization becomes a bureaucracy," he said of the Sierra Club. "The higher up in the organization you go, the impulse is to protect each other, to protect funding, to protect political access rather than to take a stand. The founding principles of the Sierra Club were to protect the wild places of the earth."

At times, when he considers the forces arrayed against him, Andy feels like that little child who used to climb the oaks and maples in and around his home in Bloomington. The two Forest Service regions in which the central hardwoods lie have combined budgets of several million dollars and staffs of perhaps two thousand, he figures. "I have maybe forty people to call on, and we're paying the taxes to support the people we're fighting," he says. "It's really quite overwhelming, what we're up against. But we do have a couple of things going for us. Number one is public sympathy. And number two, we're right. We know we're working for the survival of the planet. I know that sounds grandiose. But it really is what gets us up in the morning and keeps us going through long, sometimes very frustrating, very overwhelming days."

❧ ❧ ❧ ❧

SUE LYNCH

Sue Lynch was a naive farm wife when she learned in 1982 that Waste Management was dumping benzene and other toxic chemicals in the Wheeler Landfill adjacent to her home. Her naiveté rapidly transformed into sophistication as she evolved from concerned landowner to environmental activist to enemy of the nation's largest waste processor. Sue organized PAHLS (People Against Hazardous Landfill Sites), rallied the tiny town of Wheeler against the waste giant's plans for their dump, and in less than a year had ended Waste Management's quest to turn the Wheeler Landfill into one of the region's largest toxic-waste dumps. Sue has been the executive director of PAHLS from day one and has developed the organization into a "larger than local" group of national stature, acquiring a national reputation herself in the process. Sue and PAHLS have maintained their focus on Waste Management and serve as a resource for environmental and citizen groups nationwide fighting the company. Sue, fifty-two, lives on a Porter County farm with her husband, Jim.

Fighting Garbage Men in Suits

✹ ✹ ✹ ✹

2 Were it not for a boneheaded move by Waste Management back in January 1983, Sue Lynch might very well be just another environmentalist today.

Up to that time, Sue, then Sue Greer, had been a fledgling environmental activist trying to figure out a way to stop the Oak Brook, Illinois, waste giant from dumping toxic waste in a landfill adjacent to her farm in Wheeler, a tiny agricultural town of six hundred in northwestern Indiana. She had been at it with limited success for three years when she saw EPA whistle-blower William Sanjour one morning on the "Today Show." She decided to invite him to come to northwest Indiana to speak and gave him a call.

Sanjour agreed, and Sue reserved a meeting room at the Holiday Inn in Portage, advertised in local media, and bought him a $700 plane ticket. But when she called to make the final arrangements, Sanjour, facing pressure from his bosses at EPA, told her there was no way he was going to risk his job any further by speaking in Indiana. Mortified, Sue cried for two hours, called him back, and said, "Look, you can't leave me stranded like this. I've got to bring somebody out here." Sanjour then gave her the name of a colleague of his, assistant to the head of EPA's Hazardous Site Control Division Hugh Kaufman, whom she called.

Kaufman agreed to come, and he brought two companions with him—Jon Alpert and Mary Ann Delao, freelance producers for the "Today Show." Sue held her meeting, Kaufman spoke to a crowd of four hundred, and she decided that the next day she would take Kaufman and company on a tour of the landfill. As the group began, Sue saw that the "Today Show" folks were disappointed. "They were looking for sensationalism," she says. "There were no three-headed cows or pigs with four eyes, so they thought, 'This is really boring, why did we come here?' They were ready to pack up their bags and leave. Until this little incident."

Sue had made arrangements for the tour, but Waste Management officials were expecting only Kaufman and the local folks. When the "Today Show" crew showed up with them, the landfill people panicked. "They locked the gates when we came," she says. "This guy came out, and he had this paper in his hand, and he was just shaking as he read it. He says, 'The "Today Show" people are impostors. We're not going to allow impostors into the landfill. This is nothing more than a gimmick.'"

Needless to say, Alpert was infuriated at being called an impostor, and he became determined that something was going to air. He called New York, New York called Oak Brook, and eventually Waste Management agreed to talk with him. The result was a lengthy segment on the "Today Show." Ultimately, Sue would end up appearing twice on the "Today Show" and once on the "Donahue" show, talking about Waste Management and the Wheeler Landfill.

"That's how we ended up on national television, which gave us a tremendous boost," Sue says. "Had Waste Management not gone through all that silliness, had they opened the gate and let us in, nothing would have really happened. We might not have ever made it on the 'Today Show.'"

⊰ ⊰ ⊰ ⊰

Had Waste Management not started dumping toxic by-products from the nearby refineries, steel mills, and other northwest Indiana industries in Sue Lynch's back yard, she likely would have continued what to that point had been a rather Rockwellian existence. She was born and raised in Wheeler and went to Wheeler High. She was outgoing, a tomboy, into sports and cheerleading. When she graduated in 1961, Sue did "the All-American thing," as she puts it. She got married, she had children, she PTA'd, she carpooled. And for the better part of twenty years, she worked part-time off and on at the local Farm Bureau Co-op.

That's where Sue was in 1980 when a man she had never seen before came in and asked if anyone was interested in the fact that tanker trucks were pouring toxic waste "into the hole at the end of town." "The hole," as the guy put it, was an old landfill that had been permitted since 1971 but had never been used, at least as far as local residents knew. It was located adjacent to Sue's farm. "I followed him," she says. "I got out of my chair and I said to him, 'I'm interested. I live next to that hole. I don't know what you're talking about.' He said he didn't really know a lot about it, but he felt that I needed to talk to somebody like the Izaak Walton League."

Toxic waste wasn't something many people knew much about in 1980. But what Sue did know was that her family was drinking water that came from a sixty-foot-deep well less than a quarter-mile from where the toxics were being dumped, and her cattle were grazing right up to the landfill's fence line. She was worried. She sought help in January 1981 from the Miller Chapter of the Izaak Walton League. But they didn't really know any more about toxic waste than she did. As the months went by, however, she began to hear bits and pieces about a woman named Lois Gibbs and a place called Love Canal. She called Lois Gibbs, and she decided to call an attorney.

By chance, Sue dialed the number of Hobart attorney Jeff Cefali, who appeared quite concerned about her tale and said he would get back with her. Sue thought she was getting the old "Don't call me, I'll call you" treatment. But he did call back, and he gave her the names and addresses of several environmental organizations that he felt could help her learn what was happening in her back yard.

Sue wrote to several of these groups and started receiving information on toxic waste almost on a daily basis, not so much as to overwhelm, but just enough that her education was manageable. She also ran into more and more people who were worried about what was going on in the hole at the end of town, people who were concerned about the horrible smells emanating from it, smells that were getting worse each day.

Waste Management in the mid-1970s had rather quietly gotten the Wheeler Landfill permit through a transfer approved by the Indiana State Board of Health. Located in a rural area, within minutes of the Borman Expressway, the Indiana Toll Road, Interstate 65, and U.S. 30, the landfill couldn't have been more conveniently located for a company looking to dump industrial waste generated by northwest Indiana industries. Waste Management had begun operating the landfill full-time in 1980 and was dumping hazardous waste in an eleven-acre section known as Area #1. According to state records, the landfilled materials included decanted tank-car sludge, degreasing solvents, ash, and contaminated soils. In 1982, 25,000 cubic yards of hazardous materials were dumped there. "The benzene was very strong," Sue says. "I couldn't open my windows because the smell was so bad. It gave you a horrid headache."

Sue made two phone calls seeking help. She called her congressman, Democrat Floyd Fithian, who she says basically told her to "be a good dog" and live with it. And she called the State Board of Health, which had jurisdiction over landfills at that time. In November 1981, just about a year after the mysterious stranger had walked into the co-op, thirty-five people, many of whom Sue had never even seen before, crammed into her living room to hear what a health board representative had to say about the Wheeler Landfill. He told them no more than he had to, essentially that the facility could accept Resource Conservation and Recovery Act (RCRA) waste on a permit-by-permit basis. "We didn't even know what RCRA was," Sue says. "After he left, we tried to look it up in the dictionary! He failed to tell us a lot. He gave us just enough information to leave us hanging when he left. Then we decided that we needed to have a town meeting."

The idea of a town meeting in Wheeler was hilarious, Sue says. She's certain that there had never been such a thing there. But she and others put up fliers all around town announcing the meeting, which was to be held in the Wheeler Fire Station in May 1982. The building was packed, with the crowd overflowing outside into the driveway. Waste Management sent observers.

Sue distinctly remembers what turned out to be a prophetic moment when one of the guys who had helped to organize the meeting, a steelworker, stood up and said, "Anyone who wants to spend the next ten years fighting a dump, step forward." While none of them took the question seriously, several did stand up. The core of what would become one of the most effective environmental groups in the state, People Against Hazardous Landfill Sites (PAHLS), had come together.

Sue and her pals had no way to fathom the daunting nature of the tasks they were preparing to undertake.

First there was the immensity of the overall problem they were about to tackle. They were readying themselves to fight pollution not just in the most polluted corner of the state of Indiana, but in one of the most polluted corners of the entire planet.

As reported by the Gary *Post-Tribune* in December 1992, the sheer quantity and toxicity of industrial by-products in the northwestern Indiana counties of Lake, Porter, and LaPorte is staggering. In those three counties, which form the state's Lake Michigan border, ninety-five industries have to make emissions reports to the U.S. Environmental Protection Agency's Toxic Release Inventory (TRI). Among them is East Chicago's Inland Steel, which itself reports more toxic releases than do twenty-seven states, more than twice what is reported by the state of New Jersey.

Other major polluters include Bethlehem Steel's plant at Burns Harbor; the U.S. Steel Group's Gary Works; the Amoco Oil Company's refinery in Whiting; a number of iron foundries; the American Maize Company, a corn-milling firm in Hammond; and the Keil Division of the Ferro Corporation, a producer of industrial organic chemicals in Hammond. Even comparatively pristine Valparaiso, where heavy industry plays a minor role in the local economy, has eleven facilities that produced 366,055 tons of toxic waste in 1990.

According to the 1990 TRI, Lake County was the eighth most toxic county in the country, with 67.7 million tons of toxic materials either released into the environment or transferred to other locations, such as the Wheeler Landfill. Even if Lake County's steel mills closed down, the 8.7 million tons of toxic releases by the county's other fifty polluting industries would make the county the 105th worst in the country. Porter County ranked 122nd and LaPorte 252nd on the inventory. Tenth was upwind Cook County, Illinois. Between 1987 and 1990, industries in the three-county region released 353 million pounds of toxic chemicals into the environment, 496 pounds for every man, woman, and child in the area.

During that same three-year period, northwest Indiana industries produced 57.3 million pounds of the seventeen chemicals targeted by the EPA for reduction, 80 pounds per human being living there. More than 38 million pounds were released into the air, with 15 million dumped into sewage systems, landfills, or other off-site facilities.

Among the most toxic of the chemicals produced in northwest Indiana is benzene, a colorless liquid derived from coal used to make gasoline. It is an effective solvent and a useful element in the manufacture of other chemicals. Many scientists believe there are no safe levels of benzene exposure. It is linked to a wide variety of health problems, including dizziness, convulsions, and death in cases of short-term, intense exposure. Long-term exposure has been linked to reproductive and fertility problems, birth defects, blood diseases such as leukemia and aplastic anemia, and a breakdown in the ability of bone marrow to produce healthy red blood cells. Between 1987 and 1989, 11.5 percent of the benzene releases in the country came from Lake and Porter counties. Most of those came from coke ovens at the region's steel plants.

While it is difficult to prove a direct cause-effect relationship between pollution and health effects, northwest Indiana's statistics are ominous. Between 1983 and 1987, the three counties had 634 more cancer deaths—2 per week—than would have been predicted according to figures from the American Cancer Institute, as reported by the *Post-Tribune*.

As awesome as the breadth of the environmental problems that exist in northwest Indiana was the power of the adversary the PAHLS group had chosen to challenge, Waste Management Inc.

According to a December 1988 article in *Forbes* magazine, Waste Management in 1987 had revenues of $2.8 billion, roughly 10 percent of the total waste market. That year the company had enjoyed a 42 percent rise in profits, down somewhat from the 47 percent increase experienced the year before. In 1988, the company was doing business in 350 of the country's 500 largest markets, with pickups reported at 7 million homes and 558,000 businesses in 800 communities. Company president Phillip Rooney confidently told the magazine, "We want to offer our services to every market in the country."

To aid in that grandiose scheme, Waste Management had employed some heavy hitters to help make its motto, "Helping the world dispose of its problems," a household phrase. Among the Waste Management lobbyists in Washington, D.C., were a former acting director for the Environmental Defense Fund, a former senior lawyer for the Natural Resources Defense Council, and a former Senate staffer who helped write the Clean Water, Clean Air, and Superfund acts.

With such high-powered help, the company has established a reputation in many quarters as an environmentally responsible and businesslike partner in the waste business. A Houston waste management department official told *Forbes:* "I would rate them as excellent. They meet every letter of the contract, and in some instances, exceed it." A leader in the Portland, Oregon, Sierra Club was quoted in the same article speaking about Waste Management's receipt of a waste-disposal contract: "Once we compared Waste Management's plan with others, there was no contest. Their proposal was the very best we could have hoped for."

Such praise, however, is rare among environmentalists. In fact, Waste Management is seen by most as the preeminent nemesis in the fight for responsible waste reduction and disposal.

Between 1982, the year PAHLS was formed, and 1987, the company was assessed more than $30 million in fines for violating environmental regulations, according to an article in the April/May 1990 issue of *Mother Jones* magazine. The 1988 *Forbes* article listed some of the indiscretions the company had been caught in over a several-year period: $2 million in antitrust violations for colluding to allocate garbage-collection territories in Toledo, Miami, and Fort Lauderdale; more than $20 million in fines and remedial cleanup at the company's Vickery, Ohio, hazardous-waste disposal facility; charges in Los Angeles for divvying up territories with its competition; and investigations by eighteen separate grand juries over a five-year period for collusive business practices. *The Nation* magazine in its April 23, 1990, issue reported that the EPA was seeking "a 4.4 million fine from one of [Waste Management's] affiliates for improperly burning hazardous waste."

The *Mother Jones* article described Waste Management as "a worldwide conglomerate with an annual gross income of more than $3 billion and nearly 900 subsidiaries. Although WMI is the nation's largest and most advanced handler of wastes, it is also known for its leaky landfills, its convictions for price-fixing, and its violations of environmental regulations. . . . For those reasons, it has become a prime target for many grass-roots activists around the country."

By August 1991, the *Post-Tribune* was reporting that Waste Management had paid $50 million in fines for violating environmental regulations "over the year."

But while Waste Management's abominable record on environmental compliance and its propensity to write off its transgressions with a stroke of the pen are causes for concern on the part of environmentalists, it's another of the company's checkbook practices that they find downright infuriating. Waste Management in recent years has taken to buying its way into the environmental movement, trying to improve both its image and its ability to influence its own industry at the same time.

According to *Mother Jones,* Waste Management over a three-year period had donated more than $900,000 to environmental organizations such as the National Wildlife Federation, the National Audubon Society, and the Trust for Public Land. In an August 1991 article, the *Post-Tribune* reported that the company had made $1.1 million in such donations during the previous year.

And there is ample evidence that such activities have paid off handsomely. In 1987, when the company began donating money to the National Wildlife Federation, Waste Management CEO Dean Buntrock was appointed to the federation's board of directors, *Mother Jones* reported. Three years later, NWF executive director Jay Hair arranged a breakfast meeting with Buntrock and EPA head William Reilly. Afterward, Reilly weakened some EPA waste-disposal regulations that affected Waste Management.

Because of the company's environmental donations, Waste Management's director for public affairs in 1988 was admitted to a group called the Environmental Grantmakers Association, the magazine reported. The association is composed of foundation executives who study, work with, and fund most of the organizations that make up the environmental movement. A year later, several environmental activists picketed the EGA's annual meeting because of Waste Management's presence.

Sue and PAHLS on that May 1982 evening clearly had chosen to take on one of the most powerful and sophisticated adversaries in the war for the environment.

Sue Lynch and friends had an uphill fight ahead of them. And every Wednesday evening for the seven years following that May 1982 town meeting, except for the day before Thanksgiving or the rare occasion on which they were snowed out, as many as thirty to thirty-five people would meet to discuss the Wheeler Landfill and other environmental issues. They would dispense with the requisite business that an organization must attend to, and then anyone with new information would share it with the group.

"That way, if there were thirty-five of us at that meeting, thirty-five people would know something that maybe only one or two of us knew when we got to the meeting," Sue says. Then they would take that information and spread it throughout the community as they went about their daily routines.

Brainstorming sessions, such as the one in June 1982 on what to call the organization, were always included in the meetings. The name PAHLS was chosen, with the *H* shaped like a large red diamond, symbolizing hazardous waste, to emphasize that part of the group's focus. PAHLS incorporated the next month.

PAHLS started working in Porter County, focusing on the Wheeler Landfill. But after the "Today Show" appearance in 1983, people from other areas faced with similar situations began calling for advice. And even though most of the PAHLS folks worked regular jobs, they would make time to drive to other towns and share their experiences and what information they had with others. They also continued collecting information, and soon the group evolved into a full-fledged environmental organization.

In 1984, PAHLS opened a one-room office in downtown Wheeler. As the group branched out into issues other than hazardous-waste landfills, the name evolved to simply PAHLS Inc., in part to get away from the negative image projected by a name such as People *Against* Hazardous Landfill Sites. "We decided that we didn't want it to look like we were against everything because we're not," Sue says. "We're for some things. So we just decided to go with PAHLS Inc. after a while."

PAHLS members initially took on Waste Management and the Wheeler Landfill by the seats of their pants. "You have to understand that we were all just blue-collar workers," Sue explains. "We had no expertise in that whatsoever. But we were really afraid because we started learning what toxic waste was. Nor did we realize the size of Waste Management or who we were even fighting. We were just saying, 'You aren't going to do this in our town.'"

To increase awareness of their fight, PAHLS members put signs with messages such as "No Toxics in Wheeler" at each end of town. They cut four-by-eight foot sheets of plywood in half, painted anti-dump slogans on them, and placed them in the yards of people who lived on Highway 130, which ran through the center of town. They put big red bows on trees along the same stretch. "So when people drove through town, they saw this whole decorated town fighting this dump," Sue says. The November 10, 1982, *Hobart Gazette* described one such protest: "The protesters waved and sometimes shouted greetings to motorists on Route 30, which runs past the protest site. Many of the motorists waved or honked their horns in reply, and some raised clenched fists as signs of sympathy."

At the time, Waste Management was accepting toxic waste at the Wheeler Landfill on permits issued on a job-by-job basis. Sue and PAHLS learned that the company had applied to the state for a "Part B" permit that would have made the landfill a fully licensed hazardous-waste facility. They decided to fight the permit.

They started by taking their case to local politicians, legislators, county commissioners, the health board, any elected or appointed local official who would listen. And while Sue says she isn't sure that everyone was buying their arguments, given that information on toxic waste at the time was still relatively new, the group got solid support from the local politicos. They also attracted wide coverage in the local media, which carried their message throughout the entire region.

Right after their appearance on the "Today Show," PAHLS and northwest Indiana opponents of the Wheeler Landfill were able to get a hearing before a state environmental committee in Indianapolis. That was their first chance to present their case to state legislators. The meeting was scheduled for 7 P.M. on January 26, 1983, in the House chambers. Sue and her compadres were there and ready to testify when the news arrived. "Waste Management withdrew their application to be a Part B facility," Sue says. "They withdrew it. They said there was just too much public opposition, and they were just not going to do it."

Waste Management director of corporate and public affairs Don Reddicliffe told the Valparaiso *Vidette-Messenger* that studies prepared with the application showed that hazardous-waste operations at Wheeler would be "economically marginal" and that future expansion was not possible. "These two considerations, coupled with our concern about the opposition of the community regarding hazardous waste coming to the area, brought us to this conclusion," he told the paper.

"So, the 'Today Show' called us up and said they had heard that," Sue says. "So they came out, they brought cases of champagne, and we had this huge party and a giant banner that said, 'Waste Management O, PAHLS 1.' We were back on national TV."

❧ ❧ ❧ ❧

Waste Management's withdrawal of its permit application did not mean the end of the Wheeler Landfill. The landfill still was licensed to receive garbage, and through the years it did accept special waste such as asbestos and hazardous waste from small-quantity generators. Nor did the withdrawal mean the end of the battle over the landfill between Waste Management and PAHLS. Monitoring Wheeler Landfill was a major focus of the group and one of the primary reasons it stayed together. "We had won a major battle with them, but we had not won the war," Sue says. "Just because they were not focusing on that particular type of waste didn't mean that 38,000 tons of it wasn't already in there."

Through the years, Sue and PAHLS engaged in a never-ending game of one-upmanship with Waste Management in their efforts to monitor the Wheeler Landfill.

Despite reservations on the part of attorney Cefali, who has been the board chairman and attorney for PAHLS since the group's incorporation and has never charged a dime for his legal services, Sue and some of the PAHLS folks decided early on to be their own investigators. They would go to the landfill on weekends and walk around for an up-close view of what was going on, a tactic that on one occasion created a rather frightening and, in retrospect, humorous situation. Once as they were investigating, two men, who turned out to be rabbit hunters, came over one of the hills, Sue says. "This one girl screamed, 'They've got guns,' so we took off, and we all jumped this ditch that was like four and a half feet wide. We leaped over this ditch and then scrambled up this embankment and jumped over this old barbed wire fence and ran into this woods. I don't think I ever ran so fast in my life. I was probably ten years older than anybody in that group, but I was ten miles ahead of them."

After they had gotten a safe distance through the woods and had stopped to catch their breath, Sue got the bad news. "One of the guys said to me, 'Sue, I hate to tell you this, but half of your pants are still back there on the fence.' I mean, I had ripped the entire rear end out of my pants, and I didn't even know it. It was like November 23rd, and it was very cold out. I had to go get my backside sewed up. I took a big chunk of meat out of there. I left it on the fence. I'm sure the crows loved it. But I didn't feel a thing."

That scare took care of any impulses Sue and her friends had to look at the landfill close-up. They decided that since Sue and another PAHLS member owned all of the property adjacent to the landfill, they would just patrol the perimeter. Not only did they walk around the edge of the landfill and observe, they climbed trees and took pictures of the goings-on inside the facility. In retaliation, Waste Management put up a fence around the landfill and cut down all of the trees. They even cut down trees that weren't on their property, saying that they could fall on the fence. "They made sure that all our little towers were sawed down and we couldn't use them," Sue says.

After that, Sue and the PAHLS people would walk along the railroad tracks that ran along the landfill boundary, from which they could still see pretty well. Eventually they turned to aerial photography as a foolproof way to spy on the landfill and photograph what they found. At first they used ultralights, which could get close to things on the ground. But Waste Management complained to the Federal Aviation Administration that they were endangering people. Now PAHLS rents an airplane twice a year, and a member flies around snapping pictures of what is happening on the ground, which has proved to be their most effective monitoring technique. In March 1985, for example, Sue held a news conference at her home to charge Waste Management with improperly pumping contaminated water into a holding pond. Aerial photos, according to a report in the *Hobart Gazette*, showed a slope covered with debris, which extended into standing water. "The same slides showed a tractor with a pumphose attachment near the trench," the paper reported.

"You can see so much better from the air. You can see a lot of things that are going on and report violations," Sue says. "You can blow your photo up to an eight-by-ten, and you can see all kinds of leachate seeps and improper design."

In addition to the Wheeler Landfill, Sue Lynch and PAHLS have had another focus for their energies through the years— Waste Management. From the beginning, PAHLS made it a practice to know who Waste Management is, who the people are who run it, how they go about doing their business, whom they are tied to politically.

"I think that probably Waste Management never had anybody fight them like we did," Sue says. "When we started fighting them, we were incensed with the fact that this company came there and we could see them doing things that they maintained they weren't doing. It was a constant battle to try and prove who was right and who was wrong."

Shortly after the fight over the Wheeler Landfill began, Sue had two face-to-face meetings with Waste Management. The first was at her home at the company's request. Sue says that company officials arrived in a big black automobile and spent four hours telling her that she should mind her own business and let them do what they do best. When that didn't work, they invited Sue and other PAHLS representatives to Oak Brook, where manicured executives in tailored suits tried to impress them with silver coffeepots and trays of croissants wheeled around a posh hotel room. That meeting was cut short when those in charge announced that they realized there was no way any agreement was going to be worked out.

From that point forward, it was total war. Sue says PAHLS members attacked Waste Management on every front. They talked and strategized about the company on Wednesday evenings. They demonstrated in Wheeler every weekend before the Part B permit application was withdrawn. They hired scientists. They hired a Washington, D.C., lawyer. They pressured state transportation officials to inspect Waste Management trucks. They challenged Waste Management at every public hearing and meeting. They contested every Waste Management effort to establish new facilities or to expand existing ones. They flew over Waste Management landfills all across the state, photographing them for evidence of violations.

"What they found out was that we weren't the damn dumb farmers they thought we were," Sue says. "We took every angle that we could to stop them. I mean, we were on a mission. We were so focused that it was unbelievable. We paid a toxicologist to go to Washington and testify before the House on leaking landfills. The word in Washington from Waste Management lobbyists was that they had run into a buzzsaw in Wheeler, Indiana."

Sue also began to read extensively about Waste Management and discovered that what was happening in Wheeler wasn't out of character for the company. She read about the investigations for price fixing and antitrust violations, that the company had a reputation for playing dirty pool, "pushing people around, stepping on little people."

Through her years as an activist, especially in the beginning, Sue has had some unpleasant experiences. Her car has been broken into several times. And on one occasion as she was walking along her back property next to the landfill, a group of landfill employees lined up, dropped their pants, and mooned her.

The most frightening thing that has happened occurred on September 6, 1982. As her daughter returned home from a date at about eleven that night, Sue heard a pop come from across the farm, which she passed off as a car backfiring over on the highway. The next morning, she discovered their three-year-old filly dead with a gunshot wound in her face. She was killed with a high-powered rifle, and the veterinarian who performed the autopsy said there was no way it was an accident. The horse had been off being trained and had been returned to the farm only that day.

Sue of course can't prove that the horse shooting or anything else that has happened to her and other activists was the doing of Waste Management. But while she says she has been scared at times, she perseveres beause of an overriding belief. "This is the United States of America," she says. "And what they're doing is wrong, and what I'm doing is right."

Sue Lynch and PAHLS have developed a national reputation for their "anti–Waste Management tactics." People across the nation fighting the company often call the PAHLS office for information and advice. And despite the fact that Waste Management is the largest waste firm in the country and is well connected politically, Sue has some rather simple, encouraging words for anyone in a position of having to take them on: "People ask me, 'How do you deal with them?' And I say, 'How do you deal with your garbage man?' Because that's all they are. They're nothing more than garbage men in suits. And I think they can be beaten down just as easily as anyone else can."

The Wheeler Landfill closed in January 1993, six and a half months after PAHLS turned ten. Sue couldn't help but remember her friend's challenge to anyone who wanted to "spend the next ten years fighting a dump." "I would never, ever have thought," she says. "I mean, we laughed when he said that because we thought it was a joke. The people in PAHLS I don't think ever had any goals and visions of going into the business of becoming an environmental organization or helping other groups. We have just always done what came natural."

As an organization, PAHLS grew quickly from the time it was formed. Shortly after opening its Wheeler office in 1984, PAHLS expanded, renting two more rooms in the same building. In 1988 it moved to downtown Valparaiso, the Porter County seat. Sue says the new office provided more room for the group's ever-expanding library, which was opened to the public, gave it more visibility, and was conveniently located near the courthouse and Valparaiso University.

PAHLS by 1993 had about six hundred dues-paying members and a ten-member board of directors. Board members can serve no more than two consecutive two-year terms. They then can serve on a six-member advisory board before being eligible again to serve on the board. Board members are mostly from northwest Indiana, though some come from other parts of the state. They meet four times a year.

Sue has been the executive director of PAHLS from the beginning. She has since hired Kim Klimek of the Deep River Nature Society to do their fundraising and Kathy Matthew, a former PAHLS board member, to be the group's executive assistant and librarian. The organization draws on a strong base of volunteers who help out in the office, donate services and equipment, stuff envelopes, or do whatever else is needed. In 1993, PAHLS was operating with a budget of about $90,000, which comes from membership dues and grants.

Through the years, PAHLS has grown into the type of group known as a "larger than local," evolving geographically and issue-wise beyond its roots. Sue and others have been involved in environmental struggles in Ohio, Kentucky, Michigan, and Illinois. And because of the tremendous amount of information it has collected on a wide variety of environmental topics, PAHLS has become a networking organization for groups nationwide.

In that vein, the group six times a year publishes the *PAHLS Journal,* one of the most respected environmental publications in the state. About two thousand are mailed to forty-three states and ten foreign countries, with another fifteen hundred printed for distribution at public events. And since 1987, PAHLS has been sponsoring leadership-training conferences and other types of public-education gatherings for environmental activists. The first conference, held at Tippecanoe State Park, lasted for three days and attracted 125 activists from across the country.

PAHLS also has been involved in publishing. In 1983 it received a grant to publish a report called "Debunking the Landfill High Technology Myth." And in 1993 PAHLS produced a report called "The Environment of Northwest Indiana: Contrasts and Dilemmas," which focuses on the entire environmental picture in Lake, Porter, and LaPorte counties. It is similar to the "Green Index," the national ranking of environmental quality in all fifty states.

"We're looking at it as two things," Sue says. "It will generate a new approach to cleaning up a polluted area. And it will generate support for the work we do. It will show that we are willing to take whatever steps it takes to work in this area."

❧ ❧ ❧ ❧

After watching Sue Lynch in action, you could easily conclude that she is as well suited for a career in business as she is for environmental activism. At fifty, with oversize glasses and what one reporter called "well-earned streaks of gray" in her hair, Sue talks and thinks fast, never missing a syllable or uttering the first "uh" as she expounds on any number of scientifc, political, or human subjects with unbridled passion. She carries on multiple conversations simultaneously while answering a constantly ringing telephone.

"She works at three times the speed of us normal people," Cefali says. "It's amazing. She'll call me, and she's working on a grant, she's getting a mailing out, and she's doing the newspaper, all at the same time. And it all gets done. That's the amazing part."

In addition to her energy, Cefali cites determination and personality as the keys to Sue's rise from novice environmentalist to effective leader.

He points out that when they first started fighting the Wheeler Landfill, he, Sue, and others were completely in the dark about the subject at hand. Sue's determination to educate herself and others on the issue was central to their success. "She's a rare person. She started out with no knowledge of the subject matter at all and has just risen to become, really, one of the leading environmental leaders, pretty much through self-determination. She's an excellent student. She absorbs knowledge rapidly. She understands issues."

Cefali says Sue is an inspiration to those whose lives she touches, a woman whose energy and determination are contagious. A lot of people describe her as a spark plug. She relies on facts and logic to get her points across. She puts the facts on the table and then hammers away at them. "Sue has always believed that you'll reach more people with logic than you will with screaming and jumping up and down," Cefali says. "Sue's a clear thinker, and she's a very persuasive speaker."

She also has a strong sense of justice. She relishes the role of David in the fight against Goliath and is protective of people by nature. "If she sees somebody in trouble, she'll step out and try to help them," Cefali says. "She talks about the children a lot. Here's these kids who live near, say, a toxic-waste dump. It's her job to educate the parents on what the kids are facing and what they might do about it. It takes a lot to be the David. But she has that kind of determination. She's a very high-energy person. I think that's the bottom line. She has an awful lot of energy and an awful lot of determination."

Like so many other leaders in Indiana's environmental movement, Sue Lynch never dreamed that she would end up a political activist of regional and national stature. "If you'd told me fifteen years ago that I would be doing this, I really would not have believed it. I would have laughed in your face," she says.

While pollution wasn't an issue that Sue grew up with, nature was. An abiding love of nature, she says, is in her blood. Her mother's family was conservation-minded—hunters, fishermen, and woodsmen. Her uncle is a forester with the U.S. Forest Service. "I just love nature," she says. "The pollution issue was something I didn't grow up with and didn't understand. But I found myself becoming so repulsed by that offense to nature that I think that's maybe part of why I got into it."

Getting into it, though, took a toll on Sue's life. While she knew that her family initially supported her work in the movement, they soon tired of the constant phone calls and intrusions upon their lives. Her efforts at getting her husband to stop using pesticides and other chemicals on their farm only magnified the problem. Sue learned how much he really opposed her activism through a man who had shared a hospital room with her husband after he was injured in a farm accident. The man told Sue, "Your husband said he'd like to move away from here because maybe you'd stop doing what you're doing." But Sue was waist deep in environmental issues and felt driven to continue. The marriage ended on a sour note, with her husband finding someone else who wasn't interested in environmental issues.

Sue has since remarried, to an investigator for the Indiana Department of Environmental Management. They have an agreement that they do not discuss their work with each other. And while she no longer lives the farm life, Sue does live in the country where she can enjoy nature. She and husband Jim are building a wildlife area in their back yard, and they have a huge organic strawberry patch, wild raspberries, twelve apple trees, and an herb garden. "I just like to go out to be close to nature," she says. "I don't really want to be in this office when summer comes. It's very difficult for me to come to work. There's days I might just skip off and not be here."

But regardless of her preferences, Sue does spend a lot of time in the office. In fact, she spent one entire year doing all of the group's financial work herself just so she would better understand how the organization worked.

After more than a decade in the movement, Sue sometimes wonders how long she can keep it up, how long it will be before she burns out. She has observed that some people, particularly younger activists, go tremendously hard initially and then burn out after a couple of years. Older people like herself, she says, pace themselves better and are able to stay in it for the long haul.

Still, the frustrations can be overwhelming at times, particularly when it comes to dealing with agencies such as the Indiana Department of Environmental Management. "They're an agency that we helped to create and that we are paying for as taxpayers and voters in this state," she says. "And they are to respond as an environmental-protection agency. But I believe that they are responding as an economic-development agency. They're responding as a crisis-management agency. They're responding as anything but an environmental-protection agency."

Sometimes the frustrations force environmentalists to take extreme actions. And those often draw the ire of people such as IDEM commissioner Kathy Prosser, who on occasion has let Sue know in no uncertain terms how she feels about getting nailed in the media or about some of the tactics Sue and PAHLS have employed. In response, Sue just shrugs. "We do our actions and tactics because you will not respond," she says, as if the IDEM commissioner were in Valparaiso and not 150 miles away in the state capital. "You will not respond to us unless we put it up in a big red flag and get your attention. And that's how we do it. If we have to embarrass you in the paper, it gets your attention, doesn't it? She doesn't like to hear that. But that's what we have to do. She's in my own political party, but I don't care. I'm an environmentalist first."

But what Sue finds perhaps the most frustrating is the image that environmentalists have, not just with government agencies but with the public. "Why do people still perceive us as trouble-makers?" she asks. "I just feel like people in this country, even though we've gone through generations of change, people still have trouble with those of us who look for change. Change shouldn't be a threat. Change should be something that you make for the better. It's to make something better, not to make something worse."

❧ ❧ ❧ ❧

TOM DUSTIN

In many ways, the name Tom Dustin is synonymous with environmentalism in Indiana. For more than four decades, Tom has been involved in practically every environmental issue that has arisen in the state, and for years he was the Indiana environmental lobby in the Statehouse. He began his career in 1958 as public-relations director for the Save the Dunes Council. He found his activist home in the Izaak Walton League, which he joined in 1960. He points to the struggles over the Big Walnut Creek and Wabash River Barge Canal as among the shining achievements of his career. With Tom in leadership roles, Hoosier environmentalists in the 1960s and 1970s stopped plans by the U.S. Army Corps of Engineers, state conservation officials, and powerful Hoosier businessmen to flood the Big Walnut Creek and then dredge the state's most famous river so that it could be used as a barge canal. Tom, seventy-one, lives with his wife, Jane, likewise an environmentalist of state and national reputation, in a remote wooded wonderland near Huntertown, just north of Fort Wayne.

Saving Indiana's Rivers from the Corps of Engineers

3   Call Tom Dustin the dean of Indiana's environmental movement and he will respond with a sheepish grin and say, "Old fart, maybe."

Dean, old fart, elder statesman, grand old man of the movement, pain-in-the-neck to those who see the natural landscape as an obstacle to be overcome in their quest for personal financial gain. Regardless of the moniker attached to the description, seventy-one-year-old Tom Dustin is the embodiment of environmentalism in Indiana, a living, speaking history lesson on the subject. For four decades there has scarcely been an environmental issue that has arisen in the state, large or small, parochial, regional, or national in stature, that Tom Dustin hasn't been involved in, one way or another. In some he has been out front leading the charge; in others he's been a behind-the-scenes trench fighter. In all of them, as editor of the Indiana Izaak Walton League's quarterly newspaper, the *Hoosier Waltonian,* for twenty of the past thirty years, he has played the role of ever-present scribe, recording for posterity the details of the struggles, keeping the environmental community apprised of each issue's progress.

Tom's involvement with environmentalism had humble beginnings in 1954, the year he and wife Jane ventured west on their first cross-country camping trip. On their way back, they passed by the Dinosaur National Monument in Colorado and Utah, or what was to become the Dinosaur National Monument, and fell in love with it. Upon their return to Indiana, they learned of Federal Bureau of Reclamation plans to dam the Green and Yapa rivers and flood the area that they had been so taken with. David Brower, the defining force of the Sierra Club, had picked up on the issue and made it the focus of his first major national environmental campaign. Tom and Jane signed on to the cause and carried petitions against the proposal, what Tom calls "our first real exposure to these kinds of things."

On guard against grandiose, government-sponsored development plans after that, the Dustins four years later enlisted in a fight against a similar project in their adopted home state of Indiana, a plan that Hoosier politicians had to industrialize the Indiana dunes between Gary and Michigan City. They attended their first meeting of the Save the Dunes Council in 1958, and Tom listened as council members discussed strategy. Their rallying cry to him seemed to be "Save the Birthplace of the Study of Ecology in America," a place called Cowles Bog in the dunes. "I listened to this with a hard-eyed merchandising guy's look at this thing," he says. He felt that approach wouldn't get them anywhere. He pointed out that they were up against the entire Indiana congressional delegation, the governor, the legislature, the U.S. Army Corps of Engineers, and two giant steel companies. "I said, 'We're not going to win this fight if that's all we've got to sell to the public.'" He argued that they needed to take their opponents on at their own game, to challenge their plans and show that they weren't workable. "Apparently that was persuasive enough, because I was named volunteer public-relations director on the spot," he says.

Tom served in that capacity until 1966, when the first Indiana Dunes National Lakeshore legislation passed Congress. Along the way, he got to know people in the Izaak Walton League, which had naturally maintained forest lands adjacent to his and Jane's property in Huntertown. In 1960 Tom joined the league, establishing a home base for what was to become one of the most successful careers in environmental activism in Indiana history. In the ensuing three decades, Tom and the Indiana Ikes have been involved in environmental issues in all four corners of the United States and just about everywhere in between—Alaska, the Everglades, the Grand Canyon, the Boundary Waters Canoe Area, the Upper Delaware River between New York and New Jersey. In Indiana, Tom likewise has been in the thick of practically every major environmental issue—the dunes, the Hoosier National Forest, the Bailly and Marble Hill nuclear power plants, and others too numerous to mention or recall. For years, Tom was the sole environmental lobby in the Indiana Statehouse.

But when he is asked to point to the achievements that give him the most satisfaction, Tom scarcely pauses before citing the work he has done on behalf of Indiana's rivers. "This instinct that I have, if you will, for maintaining rivers was simply a driving force in my life," he explains.

Tom's love of rivers is evidenced by the tranquil setting in which he and Jane live. Their home, built inside and out of natural materials—stone, wood, and brick—is tucked away in a northern Indiana hardwood forest above a bend in the Cedar Creek, one of only three designated state scenic rivers in Indiana—another long-fought project of the Dustins. It is decorated in antiques and has cathedral ceilings and expansive windows that provide a spectacular view of the surrounding seventy-eight acres of their woods and pastures and floodplain. Books can be seen everywhere.

Looking comfortable in cotton pants and a red and black flannel shirt, his reading glasses firmly secured atop his bald head, Tom Dustin is seldom lacking for words to relate his lifelong struggle to protect Indiana's waterways. As he speaks, in a gravelly voice that is often interrupted by a smoker's cough, a red-bellied woodpecker alights on a bird feeder outside the kitchen window, oblivious to the riverine history lesson that is about to transpire inside the Dustin home.

Tom was president of the Indiana Ikes and Roy Crockett was the immediate past president in 1965 when Crockett first set eyes on the Big Walnut Creek Valley. An Indianapolis high-school science teacher had told him about the area, which is thirty-five miles west of Indianapolis to the north of U.S. 36. While he was not a biologist, Crockett was immediately struck by the valley's unusual natural beauty. When he learned of plans by the Corps of Engineers to dam Big Walnut Creek and create a reservoir, he immediately got in touch with Dustin and told him that they needed to get down there and investigate. "We went down there to this spectacularly wonderful place," Tom says. "It was a plant community that was like on another planet, a living library of nature." The two then arranged a field trip to Big Walnut with ecologists Robert Petty from Wabash College and Alton Lindsey from Purdue.

Following that trip, Tom described the valley in the September 1965 issue of the *Waltonian* as "an extraordinary combination of plant and bird life and geological formations, similar to only one or two other sites in the state. . . . High-ground heron rookeries were also discovered, along with extensive evidence of pileated woodpeckers." Petty confirmed the largest eastern hemlock tree in Indiana there, thirty-one inches in diameter four feet from the ground, and noted that the valley is one of only twelve sites in the state outside the Sugar Creek Valley where hemlocks grow naturally. The valley also contained spectacular stands of Canada yew, one of the few sites in the state where it is native, and Solomon's seal unlike any Tom had ever imagined. "I have them all over my property here, and they're maybe knee high," he says. "There were Solomon's seals there that arched up over six feet, over the top of my head. This was something especially remarkable, nothing like it that I'd ever seen, anyplace."

In the December 1965 *Waltonian*, Petty said that the particular topography of Big Walnut Valley—dramatic bluffs and ridges, similar to those along the Sugar Creek at Turkey Run and Shades state parks—was the result of extensive erosion by glacial meltwater some fifteen thousand years ago. Its unique plant and animal habitat was created by a microenvironment that he described as "cooler-wetter" than the surrounding upland. Organisms found in Big Walnut were normally associated with more northern climates.

The proposed reservoir would have flooded between eight hundred and a thousand acres of Big Walnut Valley, Tom recalls, which would have been disastrous for its ecology. "The point is that the whole ecosystem would have been screwed up because the plant life in the bottoms is so unique," he says. "The reason that the eastern hemlocks and the Canada yews grew near the tops of the escarpments along there was the microclimate to which the Big Walnut contributes. If you clear that off and impound that off and put forty to fifty feet of water in it, you change that whole microclimate, not just what you have ruined."

Perhaps the most surprising aspect of the Big Walnut Creek Valley was the fact that prior to Crockett's discovery, absolutely no one seemed to know about the natural treasures hidden there. In a March 1968 article on the Big Walnut fight, the *New York Times* noted: "Big Walnut Valley, now owned by several individuals, was not widely known as a biological monument until the league's campaign to save it, although some local public school classes had gone there over the years on field trips and a few scientists from Indiana universities and colleges had done work there." Determined that it would not suffer a fate similar to that of Glen Canyon and become another place that no one knew, Tom and the Izaak Walton League decided that Big Walnut Creek Valley had to be saved. They made it one of their top priorities to stop the proposed Big Walnut Reservoir and acquire the area for a protected natural area.

In the mid- and late 1960s, Tom Dustin and his environmental friends in Indiana were working hard and successfully to get the Indiana General Assembly to pass the first state ban on phosphate detergents in the nation and, among other things, laboring to get the Nature Preserves Act passed. They were so preoccupied that they missed some events that were happening quietly in the Statehouse and in the U.S. Congress. Foremost among the items that slipped through were approval by state government to participate in and congressional approval for a U.S. Army Corps of Engineers plan to impound the Big Walnut Creek. "We were focusing on these other things," Tom says. "We weren't paying enough attention to the dam authorizations until they were on the books." The fight they waged against the estimated $36 million Big Walnut Creek impoundment didn't reach its peak until the project was actually up before Congress.

Once reality set in, Tom and his allies drew on their experiences from the war for the dunes.

The entire Big Walnut Valley was privately owned, and the landowners, particularly a couple of the key ones, were solidly on the side of the dam's opponents. But public opinion, as evidenced over and over again in projects such as Lake Monroe and Patoka Lake, has little impact on the Corps of Engineers. "They do have the power, and they do condemn," Tom says. "They were really rotten bastards."

To get the funding approved, the Corps of Engineers was required to do an environmental analysis of the project, which had to show that it could be justified economically. Tom and the conservationist community attacked the underlying assumptions of those justifications. "We learned from the dunes fight to look closely at the claims, because they had to show a benefit-cost ratio better than one to one," he says. To get that balance, the corps analysis focused on three issues—flood control for the town of Greencastle, water supply, and recreational benefits. Flood control, what Tom calls "the tail that wags the dog" at the corps, was not sufficient by itself to achieve the necessary balance. The general recreation argument was vulnerable, as there were already several reservoirs in the general region—Raccoon Lake, Cataract Lake, Lake Monroe.

To make the thing work, the water supply argument had to hold water, Tom says. "They could not justify the costs without it. They had to have water supply. Greencastle didn't need the water. And we pressed them and pressed them. We said, 'Who's this water for?' It was water for Indianapolis, thirty-six miles and a river basin away." That was the plan's Achilles' heel. Interbasin water supply transfers were against the corps' own policy. "Now we knew that was just a hoax," Tom says. "They just stuck that in there to make it look economically feasible. We just killed them on that."

As persuasively fatal as their economic arguments were, conservationists had to attack the project on other fronts. It was, after all, a political issue, with powerful forces arrayed on the other side. State participation had been approved by the Natural Resources Commission and the General Assembly, and it had been authorized by the U.S. Congress.

So, in addition to holding petition drives and having landowners in the valley and supporters write letters to their Congressional representatives in opposition to the project, opponents also organized an effective anti-reservoir media campaign. During the dunes fight, Tom had established solid contacts with the *Courier-Journal* in Louisville, which he exploited in the Big Walnut struggle. The paper, which has extensive circulation in southern Indiana, covered the issue thoroughly and gave the opponents editorial support. And for reasons Tom still doesn't understand, so did the *Indianapolis Star*. The issue was covered in the *New York Times* and the *Christian Science Monitor.* He also got a *Waltonian* story quoted in *Reader's Digest.* And at one point, Tom got the project included in an article *Time* magazine ran on infamous pork-barrel projects around the country. "I can remember the title of a *Life* Magazine story," he says. "'Now See the Innards of a Fat Pig.' They listed a lot of things, and Big Walnut was one of them. So by this time, we had a lot of politicians worried."

With their economic arguments shot to hell and their political support evaporating, Corps of Engineers officials met with Tom and other Waltonian opponents and asked if there was some compromise that could be reached. "We said, 'Yeah, build it twenty-five miles downstream,'" Tom says.

That alternative would have drained a larger area and preserved the Big Walnut, the *Times* reported. But it also would have cost another $14 million, leading deputy DNR director William J. Andrews to tell the paper: "If we approved the alternative site we would in effect be saying that the absolute preservation of this natural area is worth at least $14 million, and it's a little hard to put a price tag on that kind of thing." Tom told the paper that the corps' rejection of the league proposal showed its "bureaucratic rigidity in its attitude on the preservation of natural values."

Both the state and the corps were determined to move forward with the Big Walnut project anyway. Tom and the league presented the Indiana Natural Resources Commission with 600 signatures on a petition opposing the project. The commission responded by placing in the record "its own petition with 2,200 signatures of area residents who favored the project," the *Times* reported. Governor Roger Branigan signed off on a slightly revised plan in January 1968, and the corps was ready to take it to Congress again.

But by that time, three years after Tom and the Ikes had first vowed that Big Walnut Creek Valley would be protected in perpetuity, the tide was clearly turning. The Indiana Academy of Science that year passed a resolution in support of the conservationists' position; the U.S. Department of the Interior found the valley worthy of designation as a national natural landmark. Following testimony by Tom and other conservationists, the U.S. Senate Public Works Committee refused to approve funding for the dam that year.

Throughout the entire struggle, opponents also kept a focus on the valley's unique ecological characteristics, the fundamental issue that had first attracted them to it. And as proponents continued pressing, that focus paid dividends. In 1970, Congress, citing the "unusual ecological environment of the Big Walnut Valley," ordered a restudy of "the impact of the project on the natural values in the upper regions of the reservoir site." Three years later, the corps recommended moving the dam three miles downstream. After that, the project languished until 1979, when the Izaak Walton League resolved against the dam relocation, and the

Indiana legislature pulled the plug completely on the Big Walnut project by deauthorizing state participation in it.

In the interim, in 1977, the Nature Conservancy had stepped in and announced plans to buy 127 acres of some of the best of the valley. Big Walnut Creek Valley has since been dedicated as a state nature preserve and a national natural landmark, consistent with Tom's and the Izaak Walton League's original goal.

"We lost every battle in the Big Walnut but the last one," Tom says, referring to the fight for funding. "But that's the only one that mattered."

⁂ ⁂ ⁂ ⁂

The December 1966 issue of the *Hoosier Waltonian* included a map of Indiana's "belt line," a geographic rectangle of the state's midsection cornered by Warren, Jay, Switzerland, and Knox counties. On the map were twelve Corps of Engineers reservoirs that either had been completed or were under construction, authorized, or under study. It also mentioned the three Upper Wabash reservoir projects—Huntington, Salamonie, and Mississinewa lakes. The map's caption pointed out that there also were "numerous small watershed and smaller storage areas and other big projects not shown." Above the map was the unanswered question, "Why Flood Big Walnut Valley?"

Given the near-rabid insistence on the part of the corps and other Big Walnut proponents that the project must go forward as proposed, Tom and the conservationist community felt there was something going on that they were missing. It wasn't until 1968 that they got their first inkling of what that really was. "Like the phoenix bird of old, arising out of its own ashes, that old Wabash and Erie Canal is back again," Tom wrote in the Fall 1968 *Waltonian*. Big Walnut was part of a grander scheme that the corps, state politicians, and a powerful coalition of business interests called the Wabash Valley Association and its governmental clone, the Wabash Valley Interstate Commission, had in mind for the Wabash River.

The plan, Tom soon concluded, had been for the Big Walnut Valley to become one of several "water storage tanks" along the Wabash basin so that the corps could control the water level in the Wabash River. "It represented a significant stream and an opportunity to store water," he says of the Big Walnut. "There were at least a dozen significant dams on tributaries of the

Wabash River going on at about the same time. They were trying to impound every significant waterway in the state, particularly in the Wabash basin, because that's where they needed to be able to regulate the flows."

The plan was to turn the Wabash into a 450-mile-long transbasin barge canal to transport bulk commodities, mostly coal and grain. The route would have come north from the Ohio River in Posey County, with one fork going north from Lafayette to Lake Michigan and another following the main stem of the river across the state to Fort Wayne and the Maumee, and then to the port at Toledo. A third fork would have branched off the Wabash and followed the Vermillion, Iroquois, and Kankakee rivers to Chicago.

Pulling off the plan would have required an engineering effort of yeoman proportions, given the unruly nature of the Wabash River. A successful barge canal requires a predictable navigational depth of nine to twelve feet, Tom says. To accomplish that, the corps would have had to dredge significant portions of the river, straighten out some oxbows, and construct a series of fourteen or fifteen locks. And, he repeatedly argued, they also needed to completely control the flow of water in and out to maintain those depths to provide a navigational season long enough to make it work.

"If you look at the hydrology of the rivers in the Wabash basin in Indiana and Illinois and the irregularity and unpredictability of the flows in the Wabash, even with these three Upper Wabash reservoirs, you can see that there's no way you're going to have a long navigation season," he says. "In the summer it's too dry, in the fall it's too wet. Unless you can control the hydrology of the tributary streams of the Wabash, you'll never have a barge canal. And that was at the bottom of the whole damn thing."

In the June 12, 1977, issue of the *Indianapolis Star Magazine,* writer Richard S. Simons called the Wabash River canal project "one of America's longest-running political pork barrel acts. It would be comic if it didn't reach so deeply into the taxpayers' pockets." Indeed, proposals for somehow channelizing the river to improve transportation predate formation of the Indiana Territory in 1800.

French fur traders are credited with originating the idea, to aid them in their portages over the Wabash route. And while Hoosier settlers took up the cause as early as 1800, it wasn't until 1818 that Congress financed the first canal survey and recommended a six-mile canal. Ten years later, the idea grew to improving the channel downstream from Logansport at an estimated cost of $65,000. In 1834, President Andrew Jackson vetoed the Wabash Valley navigation bill as "too extravagant."

The idea did not remain dormant for long, however. Suffering from what Simons called "incurable canal fever," the Indiana legislature in 1836 passed the Mammoth Internal Improvements Act, which included plans for numerous roads, railroads, and canals, including the Wabash and Erie Canal. Within three years, however, the ambitious transportation plan had bankrupted the state. Creditors assumed control of the canal and finally completed it in 1853.

"But inadequate traffic never reached projections and continual massive vandalism complicated by lesser natural disasters closed the canal below Terre Haute within seven years," Simons wrote. "Fourteen years later, the entire route was abandoned as a through waterway and no further effort was made to operate it."

The canal debacle led the state to prohibit bonded debt in its revised 1851 constitution. But it did not bury the idea of a Wabash River canal.

In 1880, Congress authorized a canal survey between Toledo and Lafayette, with an estimated cost of $25 million. Congress abandoned the idea.

In 1902, Congress appropriated $5,000 to resurvey the river below Vincennes, and then, "for good measure, threw in a survey upstream to Perryville in Vermillion County," Simons said. The cost to Vincennes was estimated at $3.045 million. The U.S. Board of Engineers held a public hearing on the project in 1904 in Vincennes but postponed a decision, calling the project premature.

In 1908, Congress appropriated another $50,000 to survey a canal connecting Lake Erie and Lake Michigan via Fort Wayne. In 1911, the Great Lakes–Fort Wayne canal survey concluded that it would cost $43 million, which was economically unfeasible.

In 1909 and 1910, Congress again authorized surveying the Wabash downstream from Terre Haute. This time the cost was projected at $7.9 million.

Canal supporters kept pursuing their idea, though their efforts were slowed considerably by World War I. After the war, proponents continued to push their cause. "Numerous canal associations organized and issued rosy predictions," Simons said. Their efforts, however, did not come to fruition until the 1960s.

Tom and the conservation community were not caught off guard with the barge canal as they had been with Big Walnut. They caught it at the beginning, in the pre-authorization stage. And before the first public hearing was held on the proposal in October 1968, they had already laid the foundation for their case, which they made at hearings that year in Terre Haute, Chicago, and Toledo.

But they also found out at those hearings that they faced an uphill fight to stop the canal, or the Cross Wabash Valley Waterway, as it was being called. An estimated five hundred people turned out at the first public hearing in Terre Haute. The Terre Haute *Star* reported that forty speakers had pledged support. Among them were influential politicians.

Senator Vance Hartke: "The memory of the tragic consequences of the Wabash-Erie Canal of the early nineteenth century—a project overtaken by technology—has too long stood in the way of intelligent study and planning for the navigational development of the Wabash. I strongly urge that the corps move with all deliberate speed in the conduct of this study and I shall persistently urge the Congress to keep tempo by providing the requisite funds each step of the way." He said that studies had projected $110 million in economic benefits to the Wabash basin alone from the project—$70 million in savings in the transportation of agricultural products and another $20 million in industrial goods, combined with $20 million in added recreational benefits to the economy. Major ports would be possible at Fort Wayne, Lafayette, Terre Haute, and Vincennes, he said.

Senator Birch Bayh said the canal could carry more than 37 million tons of cargo a year. "Unless convincing evidence is presented that the project would not be economically feasible, it is my intention to give it my continued full and dedicated support. . . . It has been quite appropriately referred to as the missing link—the last section needed to complete a direct through barge canal from Lakes Erie and Michigan through Indiana and Illinois to the Gulf of Mexico."

Statements of canal support were also recorded from Congressman John Myers, Governor Roger Branigan, Lieutenant Governor Robert Rock, and other Hoosier politicians.

Other than some units of the U.S. Wild and Scenic River System, the Wabash River is the longest stream in the lower forty-eight states that isn't a barge canal, Tom says. And the Wabash Valley Association, a Mt. Carmel, Illinois, consortium of bankers and industrial business interests that was pushing for the canal, as well as the politicians, used that fact in their arguments. According to Tom, they would say, "This is a prime navigation route. It has been used historically for that. Now, let's do it right."

Proponents tried to enlist the support of grain shippers and others who they thought would benefit from the lower transportation costs they said the canal would bring. They also rallied politicians in cities and towns along the way, touting the economic benefits it would bring them. Their claims of economic spoils, Tom wrote in the Winter 1968-69 *Waltonian*, gave everyone "the illusion that his wallet is getting fatter from the largesse."

Tom and the opposition did argue, of course, that the project would be an environmental disaster, destroying wild and beautiful places such as Big Walnut Creek, Wildcat Creek, Big Pine Creek, and others too numerous to list. And while the politicians and canal proponents vehemently denied it, Tom made his arguments that the canal would "enslave all or most of Indiana's Wabash and Maumee basin water."

In the Spring 1973 issue of the *Waltonian*, Tom ran a map of the Wabash basin in Indiana showing twenty-nine potential impoundments. "I made that charge and gave it wide credibility," he says of the need to control the tributaries. "And while I didn't have the data to show it, and Congressman John Myers denied it, that was the case." Canal opponents also hit hard on the fact that the canal wasn't needed for transportation, that adequate transportation already existed in an elaborate highway system and, more important, in the railroads.

Another valuable strategy that Tom says he learned from the battle for the dunes was the importance of making common cause with others whose interests are threatened by the issue at hand, even if in reality those partnerships are "unholy alliances," as he calls them. In the dunes, such alliances were made with old-line steel companies who stood to lose if the Port of Indiana was built to benefit their competitors. In the Wabash canal, conservationists found themselves allied with the railroads, though Tom doesn't categorize that relationship as unholy. Railroads are fuel-efficient modes of transportation, and any ecological damage that their lines may cause occurred in the nineteenth century. "The Louisville and Nashville Railroad, in particular, joined forces with us to defeat the canal, they for their reasons, we for our reasons," he says. They also made common cause with farmers, who stood to lose thousands of acres of farmland, forever.

As with both the dunes and Big Walnut, Tom focused most sharply on the economics of the canal, in which all of the other issues figured. "We unmasked all of the deficient computations by the Corps of Engineers for the economic benefits to flow from the canal, that bulk cargoes, for example grain and coal, were really the only commodities that could use the canal," he says. "And they grossly underestimated the cost in the first place."

Initial corps cost estimates for the project totaled between $1 billion and $1.5 billion. The real costs, Tom says, would have been more like $5 billion. "That may sound like small change now, but it was pretty big change then." And that didn't include all of the hidden costs that would have been incurred to provide the water control, which in the Winter 1968-69 *Waltonian* he estimated would be closer to $100 million. In addition, there would have been losses from the sacrificed farmland, lost jobs, and taxes from failing railroads, as well as the costs that local tax-payers would have had to absorb to relocate public installations and works. "It was easy to beat the main through routes, that is, the Ohio-to-Chicago and the Ohio-to-Erie, because they were so outrageous," he says.

By the end of 1970, the barge canal was in trouble. In December of that year, a resolution was introduced in Congress to shift the project's focus to the "Lower Wabash," the forty-two miles upstream from the Ohio to Mt. Carmel, home of the Wabash Valley Association. By early 1973, the corps was acknowledging that original economic projections on both of the "whole route canals" were wrong, that in fact for every dollar spent there would have been only a thirty-cent return in benefits, Tom reported in the Spring 1973 *Waltonian*. Two years later, the corps officials were saying it would cost $1 billion, nearly the amount they originally had said it would cost for the entire project, just to go from Fort Wayne to Toledo, about one-fourth of the total project distance.

At that time, in 1975, the corps formally proposed pursuing the forty-two-mile Mt. Carmel stretch, which it said would have a positive 1.1:1 benefit-to-cost ratio and cost $243 million. In 1972, the corps had estimated the cost of the same stretch at $86 million. By 1976, the estimate had skyrocketed to $390 million, what

Tom called a "staggering 60 percent higher than the already astronomical" 1975 estimate. The article that contained that information in the Summer 1976 *Waltonian* was titled "When Did Corps Know Canal Had Gone Sour?"

More than $1 million had been spent studying the canal proposal when, a year later, Senator Richard Lugar and six of seven Indiana congressmen through whose districts the Wabash flowed sponsored legislation in the U.S. Congress to halt any further funding for barge canal studies.

The Wabash River Barge Canal project was dead. And so were four smaller reservoir projects that the corps had proposed and Tom had fought—the Big Walnut, Wildcat, Big Pine, and Big Blue creeks. "No, they didn't get any of them," Tom says with a grin of consummate satisfaction.

❧ ❧ ❧ ❧

Listening to friends and colleagues of Tom Dustin describe him, one word inescapably leaps to mind—*savvy.*

"Dustin's a brilliant guy," says long-time colleague and fellow Ike Bill Hayden. "He's extremely articulate. And he's never at a loss for words. He knows the right thing to say. I think I might know the right thing to say, but I'm not sure. But with Tom, I have perfect confidence he'll say the right thing."

Tom Zeller and Mary Kay Rothert, who worked with Dustin on the founding board of directors of the Hoosier Environmental Council, agree. They say he's a master at adapting his message for the audience he's delivering it to. "He's someone who can be dramatic and knows how to get a statement in the press and an issue covered," says Zeller, who also worked with Dustin lobbying the legislature in the early 1980s. But when he was at the legislature, "he was a lot more quiet, more matter of fact. He definitely did his homework and knew what he was talking about and could go up to these guys and have a conversation with them about what he was concerned about. He had the respect of the legislators, even though a lot of them didn't want to deal with him because they perceived their interests as being elsewhere. My impression was that he was pretty widely respected."

Rothert says that Dustin was simply more at ease with legislators and used that to his advantage. "He was better than most of us at dealing with those people in the legislature," she says. "It's a good-old-boy group up there. Tom Dustin would approach everybody as, 'Okay, you're just another person. Let's chat.' He just fit in more easily."

Hayden recalls the time in the 1970s when he and Dustin were in Washington to lobby for some wilderness legislation. As they were returning to the apartment they were staying in, some D.C. police officers were rousting a couple of young African Americans. Dustin confronted the cops and told them what he thought of their tactics, and they let the youths go. "I don't know if they thought he was a congressman or what," Hayden laughs. "He's just extremely articulate, and he doesn't lose his temper. He's tenacious. And so is Jane. She's even more tenacious than Tom. Tom seems like a diplomat compared to Jane."

Tom and Jane Dustin settled in Indiana quite by accident and because of Tom's writing skills, Tom says. He a native of Englewood, New Jersey, she of Cleveland Heights, Ohio, they met while attending Iowa State University. As Tom puts it, attending college in the Dustin family meant attending his father's alma mater. While driving through Indiana in Jane's 1938 Chevy with a busted frame that sagged in the middle, they ran out of money in Elkhart, where Tom was to interview with C. G. Conn Ltd., a band instrument company. That was in 1951. Tom was offered a job at $65 a week, and he took it. Jane continued taking classes at St. Mary's in nearby South Bend to complete her degree from Iowa State. They stayed there for a year, until Tom interviewed for, and accepted, a $350-a-month job with Capehart Farnsworth in Fort Wayne. His background in engineering, electronics, and writing made him a logical choice for a technical writing position with the company, which eventually was bought out by IT&T.

The job, however, turned out to be nothing like what Tom had hoped, and within a few months he took a job with a business called Service Manuals Inc. At the same time, a position as business manager with the Fort Wayne Philharmonic opened up. Tom, who had always had a love affair with classical music, took it. Tom started his own company, called Engineering Writers, in 1953 and has been self-employed ever since. Drawing on his talents in writing, layout, and photography, he creates product brochures, catalogues, and publicity releases for technical industrial products. Jane handles the books and the billings, and they work out of a paper-cluttered basement in their home.

Tom, like just about anyone familiar with Indiana environmentalism, is quick to point out that the Dustin contribution to the cause is not a solo effort. Even though this chapter is about him, it could just as easily be about Jane, he says, "maybe even more so."

While both were among the 1960 co-founders of ACRES, Inc., originally Allen County Reserves, Jane remains the group's secretary and is a keystone of one of the nation's most successful regional natural areas preservation groups. It has achieved protection, mostly through the Nature Preserves Act, for twenty-eight sites in northeastern Indiana. She is also chair of both the state and national Izaak Walton League water-quality committees and is recognized as one of the country's leading authorities on the federal Clean Water Act.

Like Tom, Jane has earned the national league's highest recognition, the Founders' Award; the Dustins are the only two Hoosiers to be so honored in the league's seventy-two-year history. In January 1994 they were named the Fort Wayne *Journal Gazette*'s "Citizens of the Year" for 1993. They also have shared many other joint awards, typically from the state chapters of the Nature Conservancy and Sierra Club, and Jane has several of her own, including the 1992 "Conservationist of the Year" award from the Hoosier Environmental Council. In announcing the newspaper's selection of the Dustins the *Journal-Gazette*'s editors said that the award "honors the type of citizenship the Dustins display—passionate, controversial, American-style advocacy."

The very skills that Tom Dustin has used through the years to earn a living are the same ones he has used most effectively in his lifelong commitment to environmental protection. "Journalism is the foundation stone of everything I do," he says. His work frequently appears on newspaper op-ed pages.

From 1964 to 1982, Tom edited the *Waltonian* continuously, reporting on literally every environmental issue that arose in Indiana. After burning out, he took several years off, then picked it up again in 1992 and has been doing it ever since. The collection of yellowed *Waltonian*s that he straightens on the long oak table in the dining area of his home with the affection a proud father showers upon his daughter tell the history of Hoosier environmentalism over the past three decades. "It's all in here," he says with a glow.

In large part, Tom attributes his ability to get the most mileage from the work he does to his understanding of how the media works. "First of all, you have to know what news is," he says. "News of a fish fry is not news. You have to know what the press feels news is. And news, number one, is the unusual." Furthermore, you have to know how to make a case for the news you provide the press, be able to convince them that what you're talking about will either influence the way people live or influence public policy. Finally, he says, it's important to have credibility with the press, to let them know that you are a serious advocate, that you know your material.

To accomplish those goals, it's necessary to understand the limitations and pressures that the press operates under, he says. You have to know that all media, even the *New York Times,* are understaffed and work on deadlines. The information presented to them has to be to the point, has to be verifiable, and shouldn't be oversold. "You're not the second coming," he says. "If you present yourself or your story or your issue as the second coming, they're going to see right through it. There has to be a certain amount of modesty associated with these dealings with the press."

While broadcast media these days are tremendously powerful, Tom believes that the route to follow is through print, particularly newspapers. "Television is important, and I get on it quite often," he says. "But the base is built on the print medium. That builds your credibility. You'll find that every day the headlines on the local news will be what's above the fold in the newspapers. They probably won't admit it, but they follow the newspapers."

And when it comes to the print media, Tom finds one source more valuable than any other—the wire services. "When some of my colleagues ask, 'What kind of media list do we need?' I say, 'Just one, the folks at the wire services, UPI and AP.' If we can hit them good, everybody gets it automatically. And newspapers are more likely to run a wire-service story than a press release from me."

Although his work with the dunes started Tom down the path of environmentalism, it was his signing on with the Izaak Walton League in 1960 that really launched his lifetime commitment to environmental activism. He became vice-president of his chapter in 1962, secretary of the state division in 1963, and state president for two terms in 1965 and 1966. In 1969 the organization hired him as executive secretary, the first time he had received any compensation other than expenses for his work.

The Izaak Walton League was established in Chicago in 1922 by fifty-four sportsmen whose battle cry was "It's time to call a halt." The halt they were calling for was an end to pollution of the nation's waterways, both as an ethical proposition and because it interfered with their fishing. While the group today is a national organization, its base remains in the Midwest, with "50 percent of our membership within five hundred miles of where we sit," Tom says. By virtue of joining, members become part of three connected but distinct organizations—a local chapter, their state division, and the national organization.

With a membership of fifty-two hundred, the Indiana division is the organization's third largest, behind Iowa and Virginia. It has twenty-eight chapters statewide, ranging in size from ten members to more than nine hundred. Some chapters have their own facilities, including clubhouses, shooting ranges, boat docks, and nature preserves. While more than half of its members hunt and fish, the Indiana Izaak Walton League, like its counterparts in Minnesota and West Virginia, is a full-blown environmental organization. "In Indiana, we work closely with Sierra Club, Audubon Society, Save the Dunes Council, and others worried over the environmental effects of abrasive human attrition," Tom says.

The Izaak Walton League in 1922 was the first environmental organization in the state, in the 1980s was a charter member of the Hoosier Environmental Council, and remains HEC's largest member group. Three past state Ike presidents, including Tom, have served as HEC board presidents in the council's ten-year existence. Tom cites a veritable what's what of Indiana environmental issues that the Ikes have been involved in, and it's nearly all-inclusive. "There is nothing of any significance that has occurred in this state that we have not been involved in in one way or another, either in a following role, a partnership role, or in a leading role," he says.

In these days of animal rights, the Izaak Walton League, with its large number of members who hunt and fish, finds itself facing new challenges. To meet them, Tom says, the Ikes must be tolerant of those with different views, whether they be on issues such as clearcutting in the Hoosier National Forest, on which some Ikes strongly disagreed with the state chapter's opposition, or animal rights. "You have to focus on the common ground," Tom says.

"That is an absolute. You can't fight among yourselves. I refuse to pick on the animal rights groups. I don't really feel very paranoid about groups like Funds for Animals or CHEETA or PETA or any of that, even though I disagree with more than a little of what some of them advocate. We're all on the same side on many matters, particularly on saving endangered species. There are some of our members who just turn livid and spit all over the place when talking about those groups. I don't participate in those discussions."

Indeed, Tom says that the Ikes and the animal rights folks find common ground on many issues. The league was in the forefront of the fight to establish the Nature Preserves Act. "No hunting there," Tom says. The Indiana Ikes were one of only two citizens' groups—the other being the Save the Dunes Council—credited in the first National Park Service brochure on the Indiana Dunes National Lakeshore as responsible for creation of the park on Lake Michigan. "The important thing for the conservation and environmental movements in the state is not to focus on the differences but on the common ground," he says. "If they do that, they're going to be okay."

TERRI MOORE

There is probably no more remarkable an example of an average citizen's transformation into a successful environmental activist anywhere in the country than Terri Moore. Terri was a politically unsophisticated housewife in the tiny agricultural town of Center Point near Terre Haute when she learned in 1988 that a landfill was being planned adjacent to her home. After rallying the entire county into a group called HOPE of Clay County and stopping the landfill, she learned that the nearby county landfill was accepting out-of-state trash. She rallied her friends and neighbors, spending fourteen and a half months with them organized as a group called Dump Patrol, documenting the East Coast trash that was being dumped in Center Point. She testified before Congress and ultimately stopped the flow of out-of-state garbage into her town. Terri, forty, still lives in Center Point with husband John and children Brandon and Breanna.

TERRI MOORE

Stopping Out-of-State Waste

※ ※ ※ ※ 4 Terri Moore will tell you without hesitation that she is one of the most unlikely candidates in the state of Indiana, or in any other state, for that matter, to become an environmentalist of national reputation. Before September 1988, the most daring public activity she had ever engaged in was serving as a La Leche League leader. She had no yearning for the spotlight. She was content raising her children in the comfortable and familiar surroundings of the tiny west-central Indiana town of Center Point. Terri had grown up in nearby Brazil, one of five children in a broken family that moved, she guesses, fourteen times or so during her childhood. And even though none of the moves were very far, she found them unsettling. Her life goal was to have a home "where the kids would grow up and where being at home would be a real big treat for them."

For eight years she and husband John had shared a fantasy about where that place would be—a pleasant frame house that sat about a mile west of Center Point on a five-acre lake, the site of an old abandoned strip mine. They knew the Center Point Landfill was less than a mile to the northeast of the home, but it didn't matter. The landfill was rather small, on the other side of the narrow lake, and there were plenty of trees between it and the house, which made it seem part of another world.

Terri and John both worked in the Moore family business just north of Center Point. Nearly every day they would drive past the house and talk about buying it someday, never really expecting the dream to come true. In 1988, however, the house, along with forty-nine acres of land, came on the market, and Terri and John bought it. "We didn't know of a nicer house, even though it was older," she says. "It's got two bathrooms and closets. For us, it was a huge step up. And to have the land was just really wonderful. It was all that I would ever want. All I ever wanted was just a nice, simple home in a beautiful setting."

Before having the children—Brandon and Breanna, ages nine and five when the dream home was purchased—Terri had worked in a hospital as a lab technician. After Brandon was born, she cut back to part-time, working for John's family, who had a successful business marketing petroleum products in the predominantly agricultural area.

After nearly a year in her idyllic surroundings, Terri Moore was as content as she'd ever been in her thirty-two years on earth when John came home on the afternoon of September 11, 1988. "He said, 'I've got some really bad news. There are some monitoring wells on the back property,'" she says. "We already knew there was a landfill in existence, but across the street and down the road, so to speak. 'So,' he said, 'it's got to be somebody trying to site a landfill.'"

Terri sensed that her world was crashing in around her when the property's owner told her and John that he didn't know who it was that wanted to buy the 200-acre plot. He was dealing with a middleman who wouldn't say who wanted it or what they wanted it for. But, he told them, he suspected that it was for a landfill. "What happened from that minute on was a nonstop vigil on my part to try and determine what was happening back there, if it was a landfill being developed and who was developing it," Terri says. She didn't have the slightest inkling at that point that that vigil would become an epic journey into environmental activism, a sojourn that at times seemed to be guided by divine providence.

Not knowing where to start, she remembered that earlier that summer some men in a van had been surveying in the area. When she asked if they were surveying for the county, they just said yes. All she remembered was that the engineering company they worked for was located in Indianapolis and had a name with three initials.

While visiting her mother in Indianapolis a week after John had first noticed the monitoring wells, Terri decided to look up engineering firms in the phone book. What she found was page after page of companies, dozens with three-initial names. She decided to take a chance and randomly picked a number and dialed it. "I asked if I could speak to the engineer in charge of a project in Clay County. And she said, 'Oh, that would be so and so.' So she hooks me up to this guy, and he tells me that yes, in fact, the property is being developed for a landfill."

Even though the man wouldn't tell her who it was that was developing the property, Terri felt an ironic sense of relief. The last thing she had wanted to hear was that the property was being developed for a landfill. But at least she was no longer laboring in complete darkness. She knew something, and that was a start.

During that conversation, Terri also heard the next-to-last thing she wanted to hear. The man told her that a second piece of property in the area was also being looked at for a landfill. Shortly thereafter, she would learn that another company had taken out an option on an adjacent 200-acre site for a third possible dump. Between the existing and proposed landfills and the optioned land, Terri estimated, there was a square mile of land that was potentially destined to be landfill. Her dream come true had become a nightmare.

❦ ❦ ❦ ❦

Terri and John probably had the most to lose, living right next to what surely would have been the largest concentration of landfill space in the state. But they knew that everyone else in the town and immediate area was at risk as well. So Terri decided that the fight against the second landfill had to be a community effort. First, she figured, she had to educate herself. Then she had to educate the community.

Terri's education about landfills in Indiana came at breakneck speed. She started her quest by researching Indiana law on landfills and solid waste disposal. And before the end of September, she had uncovered some disturbing information. She learned that landfills can be located in Indiana within 100 feet of lakes, rivers, and streams and within 600 feet of potable wells. "I was just thinking, a hundred feet from a lake, part of our lake is right at the property line. I was so distraught. At that point, I determined that I had to go out to the entire community and do whatever it would take to get the community organized."

Her first step into that process involved getting an aerial map of the county from the county courthouse and outlining on it where the landfills would be located. She then went to "literally every home in Center Point," rolling the map out on tables, floors, porches, anywhere there was room, and explaining the situation as best she could, including the need for zoning. The reaction, she says, was one of universal concern and fear.

On September 29, less than three weeks after John had first noticed the monitoring wells, Terri organized a public meeting. More than two hundred people turned out, what the Terre Haute *Tribune-Star* called an "overflow crowd of concerned property owners and citizens," so many that the doors of the town firehouse had to be opened and seats situated in the driveway. Also attending were media from nearby Terre Haute and Brazil, as well as local and state politicians. The paper described the need for the meeting: "Land acquisition and other purchase attempts on nearly 500 acres of land have been made in Center Point, in most cases by an unknown buyer."

"I was very nervous to speak in front of all those people, especially with bits and pieces of information," Terri says. "But I had tacked the maps up on the wall. And I had copies of everything to substantiate what we knew so far. I just called the community out and told them what was happening and said that we really needed to organize, that we needed to form a group and a resistance to fight this proposed facility."

The town of Center Point had never seen anything quite like that meeting, Terri says. Everyone agreed that there needed to be a dual focus—organizing a formal group to oppose the landfill and getting the town and surrounding two-mile area zoned. Ashford, Indiana, resident Hansford Mann, who five years earlier had successfully fought plans for a toxic-waste dump in his town, told the crowd: "It's going to take fire and brimstone to stop it."

A second meeting was scheduled, at which committees were to be formed. Terri, who had spearheaded the entire effort to that point, started feeling people out as to what they might be willing to do. She lacked confidence in her abilities to continue in the leadership role and asked Mann, who she says had spoken eloquently at the first meeting, if he might be willing to lead the charge. "I said to him, 'Oh please, would you consider being president of this organization?'" she says. "I said, 'I just can't do it. I mean, there's no way I can do it.' I knew what I had been through for the past two and a half weeks. And he said—I'll never forget it—he said, 'Terri, you know in your heart and soul and you can feel it that you're the one to fight it. It may not be evident to you now, but you need to be the one in charge.'" At that point, Terri Moore accepted the inevitable.

Before the next meeting, Terri and a friend were in Indianapolis going through Indiana Department of Environmental Management files when they ran into some other people doing the same thing. They were from Peru, where they too were fighting a landfill, which, it turned out, was being proposed by the same developers as in Clay County. They said their group was called Hoosiers Opposed to Pollution of the Environment—HOPE of Peru. "I said, 'Wow, HOPE, I love that name. We're getting ready to form a group; can we use that name?'"

At the next meeting, HOPE of Clay County was formed, with Terri Moore as the first president. HOPE of Clay County was loosely organized, based on the advice of its first attorney. It was not set up as a nonprofit, tax-exempt organization because the laws at that time would have prevented members from lobbying. It established a board of directors but had no dues-paying members, again for legal reasons. For money, HOPE relied on donations and fundraisers such as chili cookoffs, walkathons, and bake sales.

HOPE organizers wanted to establish a positive focus early on. To help with funding, they established a volunteer-run recycling center, the only such facility in Clay County. "We determined that if we were going to fight a proposed facility, we were also going to set a good, positive example in the community. We began recycling the first and third Saturday of every month in November of 1988, and we're still doing it." The center is located at the town fire station and is staffed entirely by volunteers. For a brief period a second center was set up in Brazil, the county seat. But HOPE members soon learned that unmanned sites were too difficult to maintain, and it was closed.

At its organizational meeting, the fledgling group, as its first organized act, initiated a letter-writing campaign. Members were given guidelines for writing letters to the media, as well as to owners of the proposed landfill sites. But despite their attempts to keep the communications civil, the landowners took great offense. One woman "still thinks I'm the wicked witch of the west," Terri says. HOPE also organized some demonstrations, pickets at the proposed sites, motorcades, and vigils, all of which were covered by the media.

But those were relatively few. The group's primary focus was research. They looked to the law for whatever salvation it might offer. "We looked all over for bald eagle nests. We even considered building them," Terri says with a laugh. "Anyplace the law would benefit us, we were looking into it." For the most part, however, they felt that their best hope lay in zoning.

Terri feared that she might have her work cut out for her in selling the idea of planning and zoning in Clay County. Like many other sparsely populated, rural areas in Indiana, Clay County saw planning and zoning as a threat to the American way of life. Feelings that government has no right to tell individuals what they can do with their land ran high. But Terri had learned that under Indiana law, communities that do not have planning and zoning have no say in the siting of landfills except at public hearings the state must hold. "It didn't matter that there was a landfill right across the street," Terri says. "It didn't matter if the whole county didn't want it. I found out that didn't matter. So that really made me even more determined to organize the whole community."

To sell the idea of planning and zoning in Center Point, Terri went to farmers in the affected area and assured them that it was possible to exempt agricultural land from zoning regulations. By the second Tuesday in October, HOPE members approached the Center Point Town Council, asking that the town and surrounding two-mile area be zoned. Before the month was out, planning and zoning boards were formed, and the race was on for the town to get a zoning ordinance in place before the landfill developers could get their permit application filed with the IDEM. Because town government did not have the $10,000 needed to fund the project, community residents committed to funding it themselves through fundraising efforts such as HOPE's and private donations.

Creating a zoning ordinance, however, turned out to be a more complicated and time-consuming proposition than Center Point residents envisioned. It took them ten months and fifty-six plan commission meetings before an ordinance was adopted. But along the way they learned that they had the power to enact an interim zoning ordinance, through which they could regulate developments before a final ordinance was enacted.

Landfill opponents set about their work quietly, as in late October they discovered that they were up against stiff competition. At that time, they learned that the developer was a company called Wabash Tech, whose principal partners were Max Gibson, owner of three landfills in nearby Vigo County, and Indianapolis attorney George Pendygraft. Gibson had some blemishes on his record, Terri says, but Pendygraft was a high-powered lawyer with a degree in biochemistry or some other physical science. "The guy was very smart," Terri says. Gibson and Pendygraft planned to name the dump the Sugar Ridge Landfill after Sugar Ridge Township, in which Center Point is located.

Guarding its work like a mother protecting her young, the Center Point Plan Commission made rapid progress toward its interim zoning ordinance. When it was ready, the only public notice was the required legal advertisement in local papers. The media weren't notified until the very last minute. The Center Point Town Board passed the ordinance on the evening of February 7, 1989, requiring that any development of more than five acres in Center Point or its surrounding two-mile area proposed before mid-September must be approved by the zoning board. Board members Roger Campbell, Chris Wright, and John Hughbanks unanimously approved the interim measure, which the *Tribune-Star* said "puts a freeze on present land use and could stop a proposed landfill in the area."

"We wish to have input in what our community is and what it is to become, and this gives us that kind of facility," plan commission member John Switzer said at the meeting. The plan commission's comprehensive plan said that the goal was to "channel growth into the residential and agricultural mold that already exists in Center Point," the *Tribune-Star* reported. The ordinance became law at eight the next morning when it was filed at the Clay County Courthouse. Terri and a friend were in Fort Wayne that day, where Pendygraft was arguing in federal court the case of the Four Corner Landfill, a hazardous-waste landfill in north-central Indiana near the Culver Military Academy. They wanted to see Pendygraft in action, as well as to see what federal court was like. Terri took the opportunity during a break to let Pendygraft know that the interim zoning ordinance was on the books. He did not respond.

Before going to lunch, Terri called home and heard that there were rumors that Wabash Tech had filed its permit application that same day. Apparently they had kept a close eye on the papers and knew when the ordinance hearing was. Terri and her friend skipped lunch that day. They called IDEM and found out that in fact the application had been filed. They requested that copies be made, and they hit the road for Indianapolis.

IDEM was closed by the time they arrived, but a copy of the 600-page application had been left for them with a guard. Terri looked through it on the drive back to Center Point and quickly concluded that it had been slapped together haphazardly. Among the information required by IDEM was a survey of nearby land-owners, who were to be asked about matters such as their water sources. Nearly all of the surveys had only mailbox numbers on them, and no evidence that the landowners had been contacted.

The strongest evidence that the application had been hurriedly prepared was a blank questionnaire that had been left in, obviously by mistake. "At the bottom of it, it said, 'Do not tell them what your intent is. Do not tell them about the landfill.' It said it in black and white. I mean, we were reading that, and I just thought I was going to die. It was a joy to find that little ditty."

From the start, Terri and her supporters at HOPE decided that they did not want to win their battle on a technicality. Their goal wasn't just to stop the second landfill, it was to find just cause for stopping it. "We were going to do research and prove that the site was unsuitable for a landfill," Terri says. It didn't take long for the group to find the right issue. In her research, Terri learned that landfills are not supposed to be sited over mines. Clay County sits atop coal deposits, and a Center Point widow, whose husband at one time had been a state geologist, had a map showing that the proposed site was situated above a former deep-shaft mine. Terri called Gibson and told him about the map. He told her that he had maps showing that there weren't any mines. Hers was titled "Preliminary Map Number 6"; his was a U.S. Geological Survey topographical map. Neither was definitive.

HOPE was able to obtain copies of Wabash Tech's drilling logs and maps and hired a geologist to review them. He pointed out that an air pocket had been hit eighty-five feet below the proposed site. That reinforced HOPE's claim that the site was located atop an abandoned mine. But Terri had not been able to locate maps proving that position.

Right around the time that the zoning ordinance was passed, Terri and a friend went to the State Archives in Indianapolis looking for the maps and were told that the county should have them. The next day they went to the county recorder's office in Brazil, where they were told that the maps had just recently been mailed to the Bureau of Mines in Washington, Indiana.

Terri did not want to seem paranoid, but she had concerns about using the telephone throughout the entire landfill fight. "You can't be too careful. Those people will stoop to anything," she says. So that night she and a friend made plans to go to Washington the next morning. She called her friend at 8:00 A.M. and asked if she was ready to go to the Bureau of Mines. It took them about forty-five minutes to drive there. When the woman in the office produced for them an original oilcloth map titled "Crawford No. 5," with the engineer's pencil marks on it verifying mines under the proposed landfill site, Terri was ecstatic. "I mean, we had hit paydirt. I couldn't believe it. I thought, 'Thank you God.' I mean, there is a God in heaven."

Terri and her friend then signed that and other maps out, took them to a nearby printer for copying, and went to lunch. When they returned to the bureau and asked the woman to certify the copies of Crawford No. 5, they were stunned by her response. "'This is so weird,'" Terri says the woman said to them. "'While you were gone, a man named George Pendygraft called to see if we had a copy, and he wanted me to mail it to him, like right now, the map, the original.'"

The first thing Terri did upon her return to Center Point was make numerous copies of the map and distribute them to homes throughout the community. "We put copies in everyone's houses," she says. "I mean, it was like this thing was so valuable that if something happened to my house, we were still going to have a copy of that map."

Next, they went to the media. Front-page stories in the local papers and lead stories on Terre Haute television stations showed John and Terri holding copies of the maps. "We said, 'This is going to stop them, period. Regardless of the zoning, it doesn't matter. This is the geological evidence we have been looking for.'"

Pendygraft and Gibson claimed they were still going to develop the site. But shortly thereafter, Wabash Tech sold its three Vigo County landfills and rights to the proposed new site to Laidlaw Waste Systems, one of the largest waste-management companies in the country. When Terri heard drilling rigs on the property in November 1989, she thought she was going to cry. Instead, she called Laidlaw, where an official told her that they were taking one last look at the project. While he said they would proceed if the tests showed the project to be economically feasible, he told her that he anticipated that the project would be scrapped.

The tests showed the mining underneath the site to be even more extensive than previously believed. In February 1990, Laidlaw announced that it was abandoning the Sugar Ridge Landfill project. Laidlaw regional engineer Scott Schreiber was quoted in the February 23 issue of the *Tribune-Star:* "The mine is beneath almost all of the eastern half of the property and may go beneath County Road 32 south and beyond." While he told the paper that the site could be made usable by filling in the mine with a substance such as cement or excavating to the mine floor and putting in a clay liner, "Neither of these options makes economic sense." Laidlaw regional vice-president Charles E. Leonard said that the company would rely on the Vigo County southside landfill, which would "guarantee the highest level of environmental security while servicing the disposal needs of the people of Vigo, Clay, and surrounding counties."

"It was a red-letter day," Terri says. "But the sad thing for us was, we were so excited, but it overlapped the time that the Center Point Landfill began accepting out-of-state waste. The victory was very bittersweet."

❧ ❧ ❧ ❧

Two years earlier, Terri, like most Americans, had followed the saga of the *Mobro,* the ill-fated Islip, Long Island, garbage barge that vainly journeyed up and down the East Coast looking for a place to disgorge its putrid cargo. But she had no idea that the same forces that propelled that pariah vessel would soon converge on her life. The *Mobro* became the symbol of America's waste crisis of the late 1980s, a crisis that literally found its way to Terri Moore's back yard.

The waste crisis was the product of a clash between Americans' insatiable desire to consume, their unwavering commitment to maintaining property values, and a growing environmental awareness. In 1960, Americans each day produced an estimated 2.7 pounds of trash apiece. By the late 1980s, the amount had jumped to 4 pounds, roughly 3 of which were being landfilled.

At the same time, Americans were developing a rigid not-in-my-back-yard attitude toward landfills. People didn't want nasty, leaky dumps anywhere near their properties. The U.S. Environmental Protection Agency estimates that between 1979 and the time Terri and John bought their new home, the number of land-fills operating nationwide had dropped from 18,500 to about 5,000. By 1992, the EPA was predicting that 75 percent of the nation's remaining landfills would close within a decade. Environmental concerns had caused landfills to be universally deemed the worst of all possible options for waste disposal.

But the country was as deep in debate over what to do with all that trash as it was in trash itself. Environmentalists and some government officials saw waste reduction, recycling, composting, and reuse as the answer. Industry and other government leaders saw incineration as the solution, particularly waste-to-energy incinerators, in which trash is burned to produce steam to produce energy. The conflict left many cities across the country paralyzed in their efforts to manage waste.

Nowhere was the garbage crisis, and the debate over it, more acute than in the metropolitan Northeast. New Jersey, which had more than three hundred operating landfills in the 1970s, had only eleven left in 1992. While New York City was producing about 27,000 tons of garbage a day in the late 1980s and early 1990s, it had no waste-to-energy incinerators, one leaf-composting plant, one government recycling plant, and only one landfill.

As landfill space ran out and the cost of dumping in what space was left skyrocketed, the eastern United States' most crowded metropolitan areas found themselves with but one option for millions of tons of garbage each year—ship it elsewhere. "It's easier to pay a large premium to ship out of state than to pay the political price to expand at home," Allen Moore, president of the National Solid Waste Management Association, said in an April 1992 article in the *Wall Street Journal*. Thomas Joring, commissioner of the New York Department of Environmental Conservation, was quoted in the same article as saying that his state didn't ship garbage out of state as a matter of public policy. "It's just that the marketplace makes it a cheaper place than other alternatives."

Isolated rural landfills in places such as Center Point, Indiana, became part of the solution to the East Coast's garbage crisis.

The Center Point Landfill is located on a ninety-acre tract of land just west of the town. It was built in the late 1960s or early 1970s to the standards of that time, which means it does not have any liners or other pollution controls. The facility's permit allowed trash mounds up to forty feet high on sixty-two acres. The dump had been established as a county landfill run by the county commissioners, who leased the land from a local man named Robert Bedwell. In the mid-1980s, the county grew weary of being in the landfill business and transferred its permit to Bedwell. Prior to July 1989, the dump accepted exclusively local trash.

While Terri and HOPE were preoccupied with fighting the Sugar Ridge Landfill, some ominous changes were occurring at the Center Point Landfill. Unbeknownst to them, the landfill owner had received a permit to accept special waste, and small shipments of asbestos began coming in. Also, a limited number of trucks hauling out-of-state waste began arriving, maybe two or three a day. Terri and the HOPE volunteers were concerned about the new developments. "But we were too darned busy dealing with everything else to deal with that," Terri says.

The first rumblings of the serious problems ahead came in the late spring of 1989, when a "city slicker" pulled up to a farmer and his son and told them that he was going to buy the dump and bring in enormous amounts of garbage. "He was really rude," Terri says. "He said, 'You know what? There's not a thing you can do about it.' And he left."

The man was part of a Camden, New Jersey, partnership called the Center Point Landfill Company. In early July, Terri received a phone call from another man, who said he wanted her to know that he had bought the landfill and was going to be significantly increasing the amount of garbage coming in. He also offered her a large donation to help in the effort to stop the Sugar Ridge Landfill. Terri told him, number one, that she didn't want his money. And number two, if he thought he could buy her friendship, he could think again. She let him know that she was totally opposed to out-of-state waste coming in.

For Terri, that phone call couldn't have been any more unwelcome. "It was like the second week in July, and I was just sick in my heart and soul. I was tired already. It had been nine months, and I was tired. I'd been going full throttle, full speed, for nine months. And it became evident that we were going to have to organize to fight this now."

The call came on a Wednesday, and Terri immediately lit up the HOPE telephone tree. She knew enough about state regulations to know that landfill owners did not have to document out-of-state waste. Concerned about future liability, she suggested that HOPE members initiate an effort to document the waste themselves, a proposition that wasn't exactly greeted with open arms. "People had developed a certain level of respect for my judgment, but I tell you what, I think some of them at that time thought that I had lost my marbles. Some of them openly admit now that they did. But I just called a few people and said, 'Will you help me? We'll just do it for a couple of weeks, a week. I mean, it won't be that much.'"

On Friday, the first trucks filled with waste from New York, New Jersey, and Pennsylvania arrived at the Center Point Landfill. On Monday, Terri Moore and members of HOPE set themselves up on a member's property located on the highway leading to the dump. With binoculars, pens, and notebooks, they began recording the comings and goings at the Center Point Landfill. Dump Patrol was born.

Dump Patrol quickly evolved beyond its low-tech beginnings. Terri's purpose was to document the companies that were bringing in waste so that if problems developed in the years ahead, there would be records of who could be held responsible. At the end of each month they would record all of their information—the number of trucks, the trucking companies, and where they were from—and turn it over to state environmental officials. Almost immediately, Dump Patrol participants realized that they couldn't accurately record information with notepads and pencils. Within the first week they began tape-recording the information so that it could be more accurately transferred to their journals. Soon they would turn to cameras and camcorders.

The effort also moved beyond its initial suspect public image. The attitude that Dump Patrol members had gone off the deep end, perhaps gotten a little radical, lasted only until the first semi accident. "Once you've either had, or know someone who has had, a semi end up in their front yard, you tend to get pretty upset. We had more volunteers after that. It became evident that

79

we were in it for the long haul, that these semis were, and this garbage was, a threat, not only potentially in the future, but immediately."

For the next fourteen and a half months, six days a week, ten hours a day, about seventy-five Dump Patrol members took turns working the observation post. They missed only two days in that entire time. A member donated the use of his recreational vehicle so that volunteers could be warm and comfortable while working Dump Patrol.

Terri says that between twenty-five and sixty semis a day would arrive at the Center Point Landfill, each filled with garbage from the East. One of the things that Dump Patrol members immediately noticed, and documented, was that a significant number of trucks would get lost. They would miss the turn to the landfill and end up miles from where they were supposed to be. Some truckers did not get proper directions, others couldn't read or speak English, and one was actually cited for driving while intoxicated.

Mostly, though, the truckers had never driven on back roads and just couldn't find their way around. Even the large signs put up by the landfill owners to indicate the turn didn't help. Terri says that about 10 percent of the drivers, from day one, got lost. And matters only got worse when the disoriented truckers would try and find their way back to the landfill on the narrow Clay County roads.

Semis ended up in front yards so often that Center Point residents coined their own variation on the saying "Not in my back yard"—"Not in my front yard, and we mean it." The trucks would get stuck, jackknife, tip over, and, on more than one occasion, split in half, spilling their nasty loads on the roads and in people's yards.

One couple, Scott and Cindy Rohrabaugh, told the *Wall Street Journal* of thirty instances of trucks causing damage to their property. The power company had to move its utility pole from their property because trucks kept knocking it down. Center Point residents put up signs saying, "East Coast Garbage Go Home." Dump Patrol members made up a rhyme: "Local dumping we don't mind. Out-of-state dumping is unkind. Here comes a semi 'round the bend. Oh, when will this ever end."

For the most part, the relations between Dump Patrol volunteers and landfill employees and truckers were civil. But there were incidents. On one occasion, as Terri was beginning an interview with an Indianapolis television station, a landfill employee came barreling toward them in a truck, forcing her and the news crew to jump in the ditch. After they set back up and Terri set Breanna on the back of a pickup truck across the street, the employee came back at them from the opposite direction, leaving no time for Terri to get to Breanna. Terri screamed at her to stay put as she once again leaped into the ditch to avoid being hit.

On other occasions, landfill guards would follow people who drove down the county road in front of the landfill at night. And the guards at times were seen to be carrying high-powered weapons. On occasion, Terri says, one of the landfill owners would park his car at the foot of her driveway. But other than those few incidents, according to Terri, Dump Patrol members were not harassed. They made special efforts to be friendly to the landfill workers, and actually were concerned about their safety.

Dump Patrol hadn't been functioning very long when volunteers toward the end of July first saw what to them seemed a curious development—trash being delivered in refrigerated trucks. "When we saw the first refrigerated trailer, I about died," Terri says. "I mean, we couldn't believe it. All I knew was that I had to get a camcorder. I said, 'We've got to document this or nobody's going to believe us.'" On July 21, 1989, John and Terri spent a thousand dollars for a camcorder. They also bought a 35mm Minolta camera with wide-angle and zoom lenses.

Dump Patrol members at first were puzzled by the appearance of refrigerated trucks. It didn't make any sense to refrigerate trash. On Monday morning, August 5, however, Terri had another one of those experiences that have led her to believe that she was being guided by divine providence. "An article came out in *USA Today*. I never buy that paper, but I just happened to buy it that day, and I couldn't believe it. On the front page of the paper was this little square, and it said trucks that haul food haul garbage. They were talking about backhauling. I said, 'Wow, that's what's happening here.'"

While Terri Moore and HOPE of Clay County achieved their most spectacular victory in stopping the Sugar Ridge Landfill, it was the issues of out-of-state waste and backhauling that catapulted Terri to national prominence as an environmental activist.

Within two and a half weeks of the formation of Dump Patrol and its first publicity, a petrified Terri Moore found herself in a large committee room in the state capitol. The woman who just a few months earlier had been nearly frozen with fear at the thought of addressing her neighbors in the Center Point firehouse was about to testify before an interim legislative study committee on environmental legislation proposed in the state legislature. Along with a prepared statement, Terri had about ten photographs of the semis at Center Point Landfill.

The room was filled with lobbyists, from whom Terri hoped to get some pointers before her turn came. To her chagrin, she was scheduled first. "There was a buzz when I came into the room and everything, even when I began talking," she says. "But after I began, I mean, it was total silence. And I knew right then that that was going to be the most important two to three minutes that I had ever spoke. I was clear, I had my pictures with me, and I had numbers. I told them what we were doing, and they were just in disbelief."

Terri found herself educating the people who wrote the laws on what the laws on out-of-state waste were. She told them that the trucks coming in did not have to be documented. She told them that the waste itself didn't have to be documented. Her testimony was greeted with looks of horror, she says. "Mary Uhler, who lobbies for Waste Management, had to speak after me. And the first thing she said, I'll never forget it, was, 'I don't know quite how to follow this. Personally, I think I would rather not speak at all.'"

The *USA Today* article that Terri read on backhauling focused on a hearing on a bill that had been introduced in Congress. It didn't say who the bill's sponsor was, but after several phone calls to Washington, Terri got an aide to Representative Chris Smith of New Jersey on the line. She told him that she had pictures of refrigerated trucks at the Center Point Landfill, that they had taken their concern to state legislators and didn't know what to do next. "He said, 'You have pictures? Could we have some of them?'" Before that time, the aide told her, the only people who would testify about backhauling were truck drivers who spoke behind screens for fear of being identified.

After Terri sent the first pictures, Smith's office asked for more. By that time, she had started timing her shots so that the Center Point Landfill sign was in line with the trucks. "So I sent some off in front of the Center Point Landfill sign, and he said, 'You know, we couldn't get any support for this bill until we had your pictures. Now we've got people signing on like you can't believe.'"

Two months later, in November 1989, Ohio congressman Thomas Luken introduced legislation to ban backhauling and asked Terri to come and testify about Center Point before a House committee. He flew her to Washington. Armed with photographs and a prepared statement, Terri was the only person whose testimony wasn't reviewed beforehand.

Back home, of course, the local media in Terre Haute, Brazil, and Indianapolis had all played her appearance up big. And before she left for Washington, ABC News called to ask if she had any videos. When she told them of videos she had of maggots crawling around inside the trucks, they practically salivated.

She sent the video ahead, and her testimony and video both aired on the Evening News with Peter Jennings. Terri didn't get to see it live, as she was en route to Indiana when it aired. She saw a tape when she got home and gasped when she heard Jennings refer to the situation in "Centerville, Indiana." She called ABC, and the name was changed to Center Point on the ABC Morning News the next day.

The *Tribune-Star* reported that Terri "showed photographs of maggot-infested garbage, asbestos and red plastic bags of medical waste that has come into contact with human blood that are dumped in the Center Point Landfill." She told the committee that she had spoken with several drivers of refrigerated trucks, and "each claims to have previously backhauled meat following one or more of the Midwest garbage runs." The article quoted a Food and Drug Administration spokesman as saying in an interview that the agency had not been able to document "instances of this happening." Luken promised that there would be a crackdown on backhauling. "I can say to you at this point you're going to get action from this committee," he was quoted as telling Terri.

In addition to her appearances on local and national media, Terri, Dump Patrol, and their videos made it onto other media as well. News crews from throughout the Midwest journeyed to Center Point to tell the story of Terri and Dump Patrol. Terri and her videos also made a slot on the nationally syndicated "I Witness Video" show.

With such exposure, the number of refrigerated trucks at the Center Point Landfill began to dwindle, Terri says. And when one would come in, no matter how many other trucks were in line waiting, it went to the front to limit the time Terri and Dump Patrol had for taping.

Efforts to ban backhauling and interstate trash hauling fell through in Congress because of legislative maneuvering and constitutional questions. The Supreme Court has held that garbage is a commodity subject to interstate commerce regulations and cannot be singled out for separate regulation.

In Indiana, during the 1990 legislative session, Terri says that a record number of environmental bills were introduced, many dealing with out-of-state waste. One banning out-of-state waste did pass and took effect in March. But no sooner did the trucks stop and Dump Patrol celebrate than the law was struck down by a federal judge in Indianapolis, the trucks came again, and Dump Patrol re-formed.

Another Terri Moore–inspired law was also enacted that did pass constitutional muster. It made it illegal for a truck to be used to haul garbage within fifteen days of hauling food. "It was one of the few bills that weren't declared unconstitutional or burdensome," Terri says.

Taking on sophisticated adversaries such as the developers of the Sugar Ridge Landfill and the East Coast owners of the Center Point Landfill would have been a handful for the most experienced environmentalists. At times, for a neophyte such as Terri Moore, it all seemed too much. "Some days I just thought, 'God, don't put any more on me,'" she says, "'I don't think I could handle it. I mean, I've got to be a mother. I've got to be a wife still.'" But God had more challenges in store for Terri Moore than just stopping the second landfill and fighting out-of-state trash. Other skirmishes, some relatively minor, others more involved, also cropped up in the five years after HOPE of Clay County was formed.

First there was the asbestos that had started coming in in small amounts before the out-of-state trash and in greater quantities after. Dump Patrol was able to tell when asbestos was coming in because it arrived by rail and was hauled to the dump in local trucks. It would be double-bagged, and the landfill workers would simply stand in the backs of the semis and toss the bags on the ground. The workers wore no protective clothing other than facial respirators, which they would pull down immediately after unloading a semi and smoke cigarettes. Although the landfill manager swore that workers threw away the clothing after unloading asbestos, Terri insists that she often saw workers go straight to their cars without changing clothes.

The whole idea of bagging the asbestos, according to Terri, was to keep it from getting in the air or on the ground. Asbestos fibers can remain airborne for up to a month, she says. Dump Patrol members suspected that some bags broke, but they never could get close enough to the actual dump site to confirm it. They also noticed that unbagged items such as pipes, which they suspected had asbestos on them, were being unloaded at the same time as the bags.

Terri and Dump Patrol notified the federal Occupational Safety and Health Administration (OSHA), which said that it would be two years before any inspectors could check the situation out. OSHA referred Terri to the equivalent state agency, IOSHA, which took six months to come out and inspect. When it did so in late 1989, the landfill was cited for numerous broken bags and accepting improper materials. The landfill lost its special-waste permit.

Terri and Dump Patrol also took on the landfill over the medical-waste issue. Truck drivers had said they saw syringes in the bales of trash they unloaded. Terri took pictures of the red bags, which she knew from having worked in a hospital meant medical waste. When confronted with the photos, the landfill manager insisted that there was no medical waste coming in. Six months later, in May 1990 and again in June, state inspectors found illegal, infectious medical waste at the Center Point Landfill. Between the asbestos and the medical waste, the Center Point Landfill paid out more than $300,000 in fines to the state.

Terri and friends also had known that from the time the landfill changed hands, the garbage dumped there was not being covered with dirt on a daily basis as required by state law. In early 1991, Terri and a friend decided that they were going to do their own after-hours inspections. Three to four evenings a week and on weekends, over a six-month period, they would walk the perimeter of the landfill, armed with cameras and camcorders, and conduct their own inspections. They would document blowing litter, they would document uncovered garbage. They made up their own inspection forms, which they filled out religiously.

On the Friday before Earth Day 1991, a *Wall Street Journal* reporter was in Center Point doing a story on Terri and Dump Patrol and witnessed perhaps the worst violation Terri had ever seen at the facility. On Saturday, Terri called IDEM and asked for a surprise inspection. "I called and said we'd never requested a weekend inspection before, but we wanted one. There was a whole hill of waste they had regraded because it was improperly sloped, and they just left it uncovered. The smell was incredible."

An inspector came out on Sunday while Terri was speaking in Indianapolis at an Earth Day celebration. On Monday, IDEM commissioner Kathy Prosser called to say that the inspector had found nothing wrong. Dumbfounded, Terri told Prosser that the *Wall Street Journal* reporter had seen the mess and that she was going to continue documenting the violations.

A month later, Terri requested a meeting with IDEM. She collected all of the past six months' worth of inspection reports, the photos and videos, put them in as organized a fashion as possible, and laid them on the table at the meeting with IDEM. The room was filled with lawyers and IDEM officials. "We're flipping through these pictures, and they're going, 'Oh my gosh.' And we get out the video, and they're going, 'Oh my gosh,' like, 'What are we going to do?'" They ended up citing the landfill for numerous violations, the first Notice of Violation ever issued by IDEM using citizen information.

In 1991, 75 percent of the trash being dumped at the Center Point Landfill was from out of state. In February 1992, the landfill simply stopped accepting it. Part of the reason, Terri says, is that the dump would have been full by September had it continued to accept out-of-state waste, at least under the permit conditions at the time. The owners started shipping the waste to a landfill in Illinois while they awaited a decision on their request for an expansion permit. If approved, the expansion would allow the owners to pile trash an additional 120 feet on top of the 40 feet in the original permit. "You'd be able to see it from I-70," Terri says. "Before they ever started putting garbage there, that was the second highest point in the county. Now I'm sure it's the highest."

Terri doesn't believe that the expansion would be allowed under new regulations, and she thinks the owners know it. She believes they had another reason for stopping the out-of-state trash shipments and returning the landfill to being a local facility. "They don't want the visibility. They know that they are going to be visible as long as they bring out-of-state waste in here. They know that I'm going to be out there with my camera and that we'll have people out on the corner. They know that we will be out there rain, sleet, snow, it doesn't matter, we will be out there. And we will be watching."

❧ ❧ ❧ ❧

Fortunately for Center Point, Terri Moore had no idea what she was getting into after that first meeting when the man told her she was the one to lead the fight. Had she known, there probably would be two landfills, and maybe three, operating in Center Point today. But then, Terri didn't really seem to have much control over events. Fate seemed to direct her life from the moment John noticed the monitoring wells. "I wanted to deny it, I tried to deny it," she says. "But I guess it was just meant to be. Everything that happened was meant to be."

Because of her leadership role, Terri received the bulk of the attention throughout the various battles waged by HOPE of Clay County and Dump Patrol. But she wouldn't think of taking the credit for the successes achieved by the two groups. "It always was, and always will be, a team effort," she says. "When the people would see all of this stuff, when it would go national, they were so proud because they could feel like had they not been there, there is no way all of this could have been accomplished."

Still, as the effort's leader, Terri assumed tremendous responsibility. And it manifested itself in more ways than just hard work. Financially, the entire episode was devastating for John and Terri. She had to give up her job, and the couple spent almost their entire life savings. While there was income from fundraisers and the recycling operation, the community simply didn't have the money to fund the entire fight. "I really wouldn't even want to total up what we put out personally," she says. "The first year, I would guess, we put between eight and ten thousand dollars into it. By the end of that year, we were absolutely, flat broke." She estimates that their phone bills averaged about five hundred dollars a month, and the expenditures for legal fees, photos, tapes, copying, and other necessities of political activism were astronomical.

Even though Terri may have resisted her destiny, it's clear from talking to her that she has that combination of drive, personality, and intelligence that makes for an effective leader. She speaks articulately, logically, passionately, when she relates the stories of HOPE and Dump Patrol. Sometimes she becomes animated, leaning on the edge of her seat and pointing toward the landfill, throwing her arms up in exasperation, putting her head in her hands. Other times she speaks slowly and methodically, sinking into her brown recliner chair, pulling off a moccasin and studying it, or picking lint from the sleeve of her red IU sweatshirt as she relates her tale. But always, the story flows smoothly off her tongue like water over a rock ledge in an Indiana stream.

Terri overcame her fear of speaking to groups. She became a popular speaker, traveling often to other Indiana communities to tell the tale of Center Point to people wrestling with some environmental threat or contemplating the merits of planning and zoning. Ultimately, she was appointed by Governor Evan Bayh to serve on the Indiana Natural Resources Commission.

HOPE of Clay County and Dump Patrol both were on hiatus when Terri sat down in the living room of her dream home in early 1993 to talk about the five-year struggle. The major battles in Center Point seemed to be in the past. The Sugar Ridge Landfill was a footnote in history, and the semis loaded with East Coast garbage flashed by Center Point on Interstate 70 on their way to Illinois. The only threat that appeared on the landscape was the pending application for expansion of the Center Point Landfill. Terri doubted that it would be approved under new state regulations.

But either way, Terri said, when the decision came, the Dump Patrol respite would likely be interrupted. If the state approved the expansion, the trucks once again would be lining up at the landfill gate, roaring down the narrow county roads, missing the turns, ending up in people's front yards. If the expansion was denied, Terri expected that the same would happen, on a smaller scale, as the landfill owners would try to squeeze every last penny they could out of what little space remained at the site. And even though Dump Patrol at that time was taking a breather, Terri said that trucks would not roll unnoticed. "If we need to start back up, we'll be out there," she says with a sigh and a smile.

J E F F   S T A N T

No one would have dreamed when Jeff Stant was hired as the Hoosier Environmental Council's first executive director in 1984 that the council within ten years would become a million-dollar-a-year operation and play a central role in the development of environmental policy in Indiana. And few today would argue with the proposition that it was Jeff Stant's energy and vision that propelled HEC to its status as one of the most successful state environmental organizations in the country. During his first decade with the council, Jeff oversaw the organization through good times and bad. He spent countless hours behind his desk attending to the day-to-day functions of administering an ever-growing citizens' group, in the halls of state government lobbying the Green perspective, on the phone and in the streets of Hoosier communities rallying citizens to the council's cause, on the front lines picketing and demonstrating against environmental outrages, going to jail for his commitment. Jeff, thirty-six, lives in Indianapolis with his wife, Pam Grams, his stepson, Nick, and his son, Martin.

Organizing the State

❀ ❀ ❀ ❀

5 Jeff Stant has some news for all of those people who, usually with tongues far from their cheeks, respond with regard to the environmental movement in Indiana, "Is there one?"

"I think the vigor of the environmental movement in Indiana is high," he says. "Perhaps it's a little bit higher than in surrounding states on a consistent basis. That's not to say that there's not some areas where they are doing better than we are. But on the whole, I think that the grassroots movement is alive and well in Indiana."

Jeff's opinion is more than just wishful thinking or biased speculation. When he sat down to talk about environmentalism in Indiana in October 1992 and again in December 1993, Jeff was completing nine years at the helm of the Hoosier Environmental Council, the state's largest environmental organization. As HEC's first and only executive director, he had guided the group from a gleam in the eyes of environmentalists statewide to what had become perhaps the most effective force in the history of Hoosier environmentalism.

To support his contention that environmentalism Hoosier style is thriving, Jeff cites facts, experience, and personal observations.

He points to simple, verifiable numbers. HEC was created in 1983 to serve as a watchdog on state government, an umbrella group for the various local and state environmental groups, and to become a formidable political force to counter those who see the environment and government as mere obstacles on the road to financial gain. Within the first nine years of HEC's existence, the group grew from fewer than ten member groups and about two hundred individual members to more than sixty groups and forty thousand dues-paying members.

He also points to several major advances in environmental protection in Indiana in which HEC, as representative for the state movement, played a significant role: adoption by the U.S. Forest Service of a Hoosier National Forest land-management plan that was written by HEC staffers, establishment of tough water-quality and toxic-release standards by state government, and forcing the largest fine ever levied by state government regulators for air pollution violations—$350,000—against the Indianapolis municipal solid-waste incinerator.

As further support for his upbeat view, Jeff points to HEC's evolution in the state's political dynamic from the role of the attacker to that of the attacked. The forces against change are always in the process of trying to focus on what they believe to be the significant factors of change, ferret them out, and destroy them, he says. "More and more it's us. I think the fact that the attacks on us have increased is a sign of our increased effectiveness."

All of that is not to say that the movement's goals have been achieved, or even that it is winning. It's not enough to save the state's land, air, or water. It's thumbs in the dike. "It's a question of trying to mitigate the rate of loss, slow it down," he maintains. "We're still losing, but we're getting more and more powerful."

Jeff grew up northwest of Indianapolis, attending Zionsville High School and finishing at Broad Ripple in Indianapolis. He describes himself as an "oddball" who wasn't popular or into athletics, though he did run cross-country. He spent most of his school days lost in daydreams about being outside in the woods, where an environmental ethic that would drive his life was taking root.

Jeff's brand of environmentalism had its genesis more in animal rights and spiritualism than in concern for species and planet survival. He describes it as a sense of anger at the way the earth and its creatures are treated, as though they are nothing more than chattel. His first venture into environmental action took the form of monkey-wrenching during his teenage years. He would spring traps that had been set in the woodlots on the northwest side of Indianapolis.

"I just was enraged by the notion of these animals out there in the dead of the winter being trapped," he says. "Sometimes they would chew their legs off. I found raccoons that died that way. Other times they would freeze to death. Usually they would get clubbed to death in the morning after spending sometimes two days in the trap back in those cold winters in the seventies. It was an outrage, the way I saw it."

He recalls one instance when trappers, angry that he had sprung their traps, chased him through the woods shooting at him. As he lay behind an old log, bullets whizzed over his head. "I don't know what they would have done if they would have finally got me in their sights, if they would have shot me or what."

He agrees with colleagues such as Bob Klawitter that environmentalism and planet survival are inseparable. "But what drives me is a sense of moral outrage over the way the environment and other people and animals are being treated by people without an environmental ethic, who tend to be people in control of everything."

Jeff's early involvement in organized environmentalism came in the late 1970s when he was a student studying biology and environmental sciences at Indiana University in Bloomington. At the time, the struggle over a protected wilderness area in the Hoosier National Forest was raging. He watched a debate one night in 1977 between a Brown County landowner opposed to the wilderness proposal and Les Zimmer, then a work-study student with the organization he would later head, The Nature Conservancy. Afterward, Jeff approached Zimmer, who urged him to attend the Bloomington Sierra Club wildlife committee meetings.

From that moment on, Jeff immersed himself in the Sierra Club and its issues—forest management and the Alaska lands battle, the Clean Air Act, and things such as the bottle bill, the Wabash River Barge Canal, and the Kankakee River Basin Commission's attempt to finish off the last wetlands along the Kankakee—all while going to school. His major focus, though, was the Salt Creek Wilderness Area proposal for the Hoosier National Forest, and he quickly became a moving force in the pro-wilderness movement, honing his organizational and political skills along the way. The compromise Charles Deam Wilderness Bill was passed by Congress the same day in 1982 that Jeff took his final test as an IU undergraduate.

Rather than put his scientific training to use as a college graduate, Jeff turned to the skills he had developed, and the connections he had made, during his politicking on behalf of the environment. He went to Washington, moved in with the family of Jeff Burnham, an aide to Senator Richard Lugar whom he had met during the wilderness fights, and took a job with the National Taxpayers Union. He spent the next two years lobbying Congress and statehouses across the country on behalf of a constitutional amendment requiring a balanced budget.

While trapped in the unnatural confines of Washington, D.C., in late 1984, Jeff received a telephone call from Art Edelstein, who was on a committee that had developed a job description for the position of executive director of the new Hoosier Environmental Council. The committee had authorized him to offer Jeff the job.

Before HEC's formation in 1983, Indiana's environmental movement had been a loose-knit confederation of disparate groups with varying interests and memberships. While national entities such as the Izaak Walton League and the Sierra Club had state organizations, there was no overarching state body that represented environmental interests in the state capital. During the 1970s, Jim Jontz, the state's first Green legislator, would convene the heads of the various groups in Indianapolis to discuss the previous legislative results and brainstorm about future issues and strategies. The state group was Jontz's brainchild.

An initial but unsuccessful effort in the late 1970s was a group called the Indiana Eco Coalition. The coalition was well-intentioned, but it suffered from a lack of organization. It was, in the words of Tom Dustin, "a formless, amorphous thing that really did nothing." When environmental leaders began talking in the early 1980s about making another try, Dustin was among those who resisted, worrying that it would suffer the same fate as the Eco Coalition. But others, such as Fred Widlack, persisted, and HEC was born in late 1983 to "facilitate communication between environmental organizations in the state, to disseminate information on environmental issues to members and to the public, to coordinate action on environmental issues and to monitor state boards and agencies."

At the HEC board meeting of August 25, 1984, board president Widlack announced that the group had received a $25,000 grant from the Chicago-based Joyce Foundation to hire an executive director. The group's first newsletter, in September 1984, said that it would have to raise on its own between $40,000 and $50,000 to hire a secretary, rent office space, and pay operating expenses.

When Edelstein called him, Jeff was anxious to get back into environmental politics. But he had ideas of his own about what was needed. His view was that the organization needed a large, powerful, individual membership base to be effective. "I was not willing to work for just a coalition that was going to be dictated to by its member groups or to set up some nice, sanitary little clearinghouse of information," he says. "We were either going to get things done and become very powerful, or they needed to hire another person." Jeff was hired on January 14, 1985, and he moved into HEC's one-room office in the ISTA building in downtown Indianapolis across from the Statehouse.

Jeff's first year on the job was intense, at times confusing, and rather stormy. The board told Jeff that it did not want him involved in the legislature. But the 1985 session began the same week that he took the job, and he spent much of his first few weeks arguing with legislators who were creating the Indiana Department of Environmental Management and considering legislation that would have effectively created an open season on coyotes in Indiana.

Most of his time, though, was spent on organizational matters, getting his files in order, and monitoring state boards and commissions responsible for environmental protection. He published a newsletter called "Board Watch," through which he kept the small HEC membership informed of the boards' actions. Before the year was out, he hired an administrative assistant to help with the day-to-day activities and to work on membership development.

But Jeff also had issues of his own that he wanted to monitor, particularly the Hoosier National Forest land-management plan. And that agenda put him at odds with HEC board president Dick Van Frank. Jeff says Van Frank wanted to give him a list of things to do each day and have him report back on the results. "I said, 'That's micromanaging,'" Jeff says. "'You hired me to get things done. Let me do things my way and hold me accountable for whether things get done or not.'" The conflict led to a showdown at which Jeff and his assistant, Lori Bernadine, gave an ultimatum to the board—let them do it their way or hire someone else. The result was that the board asked Van Frank to step down as president. He quit the board.

By year's end, HEC was developing into a respectable organization, had moved to newer, larger quarters in Victoria Centre on East Washington Street, and was looking to the future.

The May 1986 *Monitor*, HEC's quarterly newsletter, laid out the group's action plan for 1986. Its four component parts—fundraising and organization building, monitoring state regulatory bodies, implementing special projects, and focusing on specific issues— provided an outline of the priorities that would consume HEC and Jeff Stant through the rest of the 1980s.

While Jeff's passion lies with the issues, his position as executive director necessarily involved him in the day-to-day operations of the organization and in building a base of popular support. In the 1986 action plan, fundraising and organization building were number one. The goal was to add twenty new environmental groups to the membership, to increase the number of members from less than two hundred to fifteen hundred, and to develop a fundraising strategy that would increase individual contributions to $8,000.

Jeff maintained his original vision that HEC needed to be more than just an umbrella organization for local environmental groups across the state. It needed to have a strong membership base of its own. That meant carrying HEC's message to the public. And in the early days, such a goal seemed distant at best.

In his "Executive Director's Column" in the May 1986 *Monitor*, Jeff spoke to the issue in two ways.

He wrote about a visit he had made to "Career Day" at Greenwood High School. "At first, students seemed hesitant to stop by. They were more interested in mobbing the tables of the military service branches, particularly the one with tough-looking Marines in colorful uniforms standing behind it. I sort of felt like my time had passed, that students interested in the environment were gone." But as he dropped discussion on career opportunities and started talking from his heart about the Hoosier National Forest, Jeff's second-class status changed. "By the final hour, my table was being mobbed with lively discussion, the only table where I could discern such was happening besides the military tables. The Marines even looked over at me a few times as I talked about the problems with federal government timbering." There was hope, even in the heyday of the anti-environmental Reagan era.

In that same article, Jeff called on HEC members to be bold in their thinking and optimistic in the belief that a membership of 25,000 could be reached within a decade. "If we want our toil to create a movement, to perpetuate our thinking and our ethics, then something more bold, more 'full-time,' is needed. . . . I fervently disagree with those who say we are incapable of accomplishing such feats. Although our issues may not seem as direct as utility rates, every poll taken indicates more citizens than just us environmentalists are concerned about the environment, about quality of life."

HEC grew slowly until two years later, when Jeff and others convinced the HEC board to undertake the group's most significant organizational step forward since its creation—the HEC Canvass. The project had multiple purposes: public education, developing statewide campaigns on specific issues, and fundraising. Canvassers would knock on doors and discuss specific issues with citizens, carry petitions on those issues, and solicit donations and HEC memberships. Canvass director Charlene Griffin, in the November 1988 *Monitor,* described it as a "person-to-person, door-to-door canvass program to spread the word on crucial environmental issues to the Indianapolis public and, eventually, statewide. An altogether realistic projection is that the canvass effort will increase HEC membership from 800 to near 8,000 in 1989."

In 1989, HEC canvassers took to the streets to talk about the Hoosier National Forest management plan. They visited sixty thousand homes and increased the organization's membership to roughly five thousand. HEC revenues that year increased by 110 percent, to $391,363, with an estimated 70 percent of that coming from the canvass.

The HEC staff by that time had grown to seven full-time members and eighteen canvassers. The organization also had moved to a new location at 3620 North Meridian Street, paying some $20,000 a year in rent. HEC listed sixty-four member organizations and individual membership growing by five hundred a month.

Before the Hoosier National Forest canvass ended in 1990, 125,000 signatures had been collected in support of HEC's proposed management plan, the Conservationist Alternative, which had been written primarily by then HEC staffer Jeff St. Clair. That plan, with some modification, ultimately was adopted by the Forest Service, with Forest Supervisor Frank Voytas telling the media, "You can't ignore 125,000 signatures."

After the HNF canvass was completed, HEC's individual membership had grown to twenty thousand. In the April 1991 *Monitor*, Jeff summed up the experience: "One lesson that we have learned is that making meaningful strides requires the effective use of the power of the people." During an interview in his HEC office a year later, Jeff expanded on that thought: "We accomplished that because we went door to door. We didn't wait on the media, we didn't wait on the politicians to decide, 'Yeah, they've got merit.' We went and we knocked on doors and we said, 'This is the case, they're going to cut four-fifths of the forest down if you don't sign this petition.' Well, the bottom line today is they are not going to cut more than one-third of the forest because we did that."

By the end of 1991, HEC had grown from a fledgling group with an $897 budget eight years earlier to a formidable force in Indiana politics with a budget of $973,663 and an individual membership base of forty thousand, sixty-five member groups, and a full-time staff of ten.

✤ ✤ ✤ ✤

1992, HEC's ninth year in existence, in many ways marked its coming of age, though it was also marked by financial setback. The canvass continued making progress, this time collecting 122,000 signatures on petitions calling for community solid-waste plans to include far-reaching recycling and composting programs. Fundraising, however, fell off from the 1991 level, with revenues dropping to $931,973.

But overshadowing that discouraging development were significant advances—creation of the Hoosier Environmental Council Action Fund (HECAF) and the HEC Legal Defense Fund, and expansion into northwest Indiana.

From the day Jeff first walked into the HEC office, his goal has been to make the organization a political power to be reckoned with in Indiana. The forces that see the environment as a means to their own ends, property to be manipulated for their financial gain, are all powerful, monolithic institutions that can forge alliances with other powerful institutions when environmental conflicts arise, he argues. Without an equally powerful countervailing force to stymie them, those institutions will continue to have their way with the state legislature and regulatory agencies. And the environment will always be the loser. "I want us to become as organized and as powerful as the Indiana Farm Bureau in getting the legislature to do what we want," he says.

With the success of the Hoosier National Forest canvass, Jeff and HEC for the first time flexed the kind of political muscle that they had been seeking. And the euphoria from that success inspired an ambitious political agenda for 1991. Grassroots director Marie Zellar, in an April 1991 *Monitor* cover article titled "Going for the Green: HEC's 1991 Legislative Agenda," laid out the priorities: passage of a Wetlands Preservation Act, establishment of the Indiana Heritage Trust for purchase of land for state parks and forests, increased funding for IDEM, a ban on burning hazardous waste for energy recovery in cement kilns, and support for legislation to improve the Solid Waste Districting and Planning Act of 1990.

The article was the first such listing of legislative priorities in the group's history. And it almost spelled disaster. As Jeff learned from Michael Mullet, who handles tax matters for the Citizens Action Coalition, an HEC ally, pursuing such a comprehensive political agenda could have been a violation of HEC's tax-exempt status. IRS regulations place strict limits on how much groups such as HEC can spend on political lobbying. "We were just sort of stumbling along, not realizing what we were doing," Jeff says. "We were growing so fast that we were doing things that we needed to be keeping tighter control on."

The answer to keeping that control was HECAF, an action fund that could engage in more expansive lobbying activities. HEC president Jack Gay explained its role in the Spring 1992 *Monitor:* "It is clear that we must have a voice in the legislature to lobby for passage of environmentally sound bills and against bills that adversely impact the environment. . . . HECAF should enable us to do a better job of lobbying without concern over exceeding strict spending limits placed on HEC's lobbying activities."

Jeff elaborated on that theme in another *Monitor* article: "To really change Indiana, we can no longer short-shrift our involvement in the Indiana legislature. We can call our state legislators each spring until the cows come home, but if environmentalists do not get more actively involved in elections and re-elections, we will continue to be taken less seriously by them than those interests that are involved."

One of the first major HECAF acts was the publication in the Summer/Fall 1992 *Monitor* of a report card on legislators' votes on Green issues in the previous general assembly. The "voting study" ranked lawmakers on a scale of 0 to 100. During 1992, 57 percent of expenditures were incurred by HECAF.

Equally as significant for Jeff and HEC was the creation in late 1992 of the HEC Legal Defense Fund. To that point, HEC had never been able to effectively use the Indiana courts. Creation of the defense fund and the hiring of attorneys Ann Long and Barb Lollar in March 1993 to direct the legal efforts were intended to change that. "Important environmental campaigns should never be truncated for lack of resources to litigate," Jeff wrote in the *Monitor*. "It is time to redirect the practice of environmental law in this state to mean something other than being paid $200 an hour by corporate Indiana to help the powerful few get around 'burdensome' laws and regulations."

Long announced the fund's first victory in the Summer/Fall 1993 *Monitor*. In March, HEC lawyers had filed suit in Brown Circuit Court, appealing a decision by the Brown County Board of Zoning Appeals to allow a private group to place a 490-foot-tall radio tower in the middle of Morgan-Monroe and Yellowwood state forests northwest of Nashville. On the eve of a scheduled court hearing, Brown County Broadcasters Inc. notified the court that they were withdrawing their plans.

Finally, another of Jeff's long-time goals, expanding HEC's influence beyond Indianapolis, also was realized in March when the organization opened its northwest Office in Michigan City. After a six-month search, Michele Nanni, an eight-year veteran of the Greenpeace organization, was hired to run the new office. "Although HEC is a statewide organization, being based in Indianapolis has made it difficult to work with those citizens and organizations facing environmental challenges at the far ends of our state," Jeff wrote in the *Monitor*. He eventually wants to establish an office in the Ohio Valley as well.

Jeff summed up HEC's first nine years: "Each year has seemed to go by faster and more furiously than the previous one. Judging from our activity in 1992, staff of this organization might characterize the difference between HEC in its beginnings and HEC now as moving beyond 'watching' state agencies and 'disseminating information' about them to becoming more effective in shaping outcomes of issues at the state level."

Indeed, such progress was noted by the *Indianapolis Star* two years earlier, when reporter Pat Morrison wrote about HEC's growing influence: "With the growing membership has come more recognition and a higher profile in state policy. Members of Gov. Evan Bayh's administration regularly talk to council members, and Bayh made a point of inviting HEC members to his office for the signing of several pieces of environmental legislation earlier this year. HEC representatives also are consulted by state Department of Environmental Management officials when rule changes or protection standards for the state's water and air are considered."

Having an impact on public policy in the environmental arena requires both an interested and an educated public, as well as respecting bodies of policymakers. It's a two-way street that requires information constantly flowing in both directions. One of Jeff's and HEC's primary missions is to facilitate that flow. They accomplish that objective by maintaining a continuous presence in the Statehouse, monitoring and providing input to the boards and commissions that establish and enforce regulations under state environmental laws, and undertaking occasional special projects aimed at educating the public and influencing policymakers.

Someone from HEC, either Jeff or one of the other staff members with particular expertise in a particular area, attends nearly every meeting of state regulatory bodies. They then report to all HEC members and member groups the actions of those bodies through the "Board Watch" newsletter. The publication over the past decade has tracked nearly every decision, major or minor, that has been made by boards such as the Natural Resources Commission, the Air Pollution Control Board, the Water Pollution Control Board, and the Solid Waste Management Board.

Through the years, HEC also has tackled several special projects designed to educate the public and further the environmentalist agenda in the state. Among them were studies on whether the state had the ability to effectively manage its own hazardous-waste regulatory programs, describing the environmental impacts from the disposal of coal-combustion waste in surface mines, and examining the state's groundwater.

By far the most ambitious and successful was the 1986 groundwater study. Using a Joyce Foundation grant, HEC hired Indiana

University School of Public and Environmental Affairs master's student Roger Davis to work on the project. The result was a slick mini-magazine called "Groundwater: Indiana's Unseen Resource," which was released in April 1987.

Ethyle Bloch, HEC board president at the time, summarized the need for the study: "This project was undertaken to emphasize how important Indiana's groundwater is to its development. Overall, the Indiana Department of Environmental Management, IDEM, estimates that about 59 percent of the state's entire population uses groundwater for its drinking water. Additionally, industry is now using an average of 602 million gallons of groundwater daily, with irrigation and livestock uses combining for another 106 million gallons per day."

The news release announcing the study also quoted Bob Pedersen from the United Auto Workers (a HEC member group); Donna McCarty, president of the Hoosier Audubon Council; and former HEC board president Dick Van Frank, who served as the group's groundwater consultant. "Indiana is the only state left in the union outside Wyoming that has not obtained responsibility from U.S. EPA to just test its own public water supplies," Van Frank said. "This has to change. Public concern over the state's commitment to protect its drinking water is already high and is bound to get higher. We need to take authority for enforcing the Safe Drinking Water Act in Indiana. Better yet, we need to develop a comprehensive policy for protecting groundwater before it becomes drinking water."

In the study, Davis begins with a complete but elementary lesson for the reader on groundwater, explaining the hydrologic cycle, what aquifers are and how they work, the relationship between groundwater and surface water, and how important it is to the state and its citizens.

The study goes on to discuss areas in the state that are susceptible to contamination, groundwater quality and quantity, and how the state and federal governments "protect" groundwater. It includes informative maps and graphs, and ends with nine recommendations that should be included in state groundwater policy.

The Davis study had far-reaching impact, particularly in the areas of public education and raising HEC's stature around the state. Somewhere between 40,000 and 50,000 copies were printed, primarily because professors at universities across the state used it in introductory hydrogeology classes. It gave the group credibility with academics at Purdue and IU, officials at

IDEM, and the media, which gave it wide coverage. But that's as far as its influence reached. "It didn't do much in terms of a policy impact," Jeff says. "We've never created much of a policy fervor for doing anything on groundwater regs. It's hard to do that because people only tend to get involved in groundwater efforts out of a purely reactionary 'My water's screwed up, what can I do?' kind of thing. We've never been able to get those people to go beyond their water wells."

While Jeff and HEC maintain a strong focus and presence in Indianapolis and in the Statehouse, their reach extends to all four corners of the state when it comes to specific issues. They work cooperatively with member groups on issues such as planned pollution in a minority community in Michigan City, an environmentally disastrous theme park on the shores of Patoka Lake in rural Orange County, a pork-barrel highway to Evansville, hazardous-waste landfills in Indianapolis or Terre Haute, or the bigger issue of solid-waste planning that affects every community in the state.

Primarily, Jeff says, HEC works in Indianapolis as a resource for local groups and performs "sort of a lobbying function at the seat of state government on the issues while they're the ones at the local levels." But HEC on occasion has helped organize groups to fight local issues and in a few instances has gone out itself and organized. Examples include the Patoka Wildlife Refuge, the Tillery Hill development on Patoka Lake, and a proposal from the Indiana Department of Natural Resources to convert 1,423 acres of Versailles State Park into state forest and timber it.

Sometimes, Jeff says, the issues are just too critical for HEC not to get involved, even if it means moving resources a couple hundred miles from HEC's base in Indianapolis.

The Trail Creek atrocity in Michigan City in 1987 was a case in point. "We camped out there for about a month," Jeff says. The issue involved the U.S. Army Corps of Engineers' dredging of Trail Creek and dumping the sediments in a "confined disposal facility" (CDF) in a predominantly African American neighborhood called the Canada community. The sediments were laced with heavy metals and cyanide "tens, hundreds, and in some cases thousands of times higher than Safe Drinking Water Standards," Jeff wrote in his "Executive Director's Column" in August 1987. The EPA would not allow the sediments to be dumped in Lake Michigan.

The LaPorte County Landfill wouldn't accept them. Neither would a landfill in Chicago that normally accepted dredge sediments. The unpermitted CDF in the Canada neighborhood had been built in 1979 with no liner and unknown subsoils, and it had discharge pipes penetrating its outer walls.

Canada residents, environmental groups from the region, and HEC demonstrated for weeks in an unsuccessful attempt to stop the dumping. On July 7, 1987, Jeff and seven others were arrested for their activities. They were released on $300 bond each. The dredging was temporarily halted a few days later when it was discovered that trucks carrying the toxic sediments away were spilling them on the roadways.

Such passion, however, fell on deaf ears. Legal efforts to stop the dredging and dumping were rejected by a federal court judge.

Jeff says that his and HEC's participation in the Trail Creek issue was necessary because it was a classic case of environmental racism, the tendency for government and industry to locate polluting industries and facilities in minority neighborhoods. "If I were going to write an article justifying my involvement in protests that have been ongoing for two weeks in Michigan City's Canada neighborhood, it would argue that environmental laws were enacted to protect all people, not just those with political clout," he wrote in the *Monitor*. "Who cares about the laws anyway? Why, Canada's just full of poor black folks. . . . Does anyone wonder what would happen if the authorities tried the same approach behind the $200,000 houses in Long Beach on the other side of Michigan City? . . . Government is making a charade out of our environmental laws, enforcing them rigidly for some, but not at all for others. We must confront this attitude and those who have it with the most vigorous of protests."

What HEC has become is absolutely the result of Jeff Stant's vision and dedication, according to those familiar with the organization.

"HEC is very much Jeff's child," says Mary Kay Rothert, one of the original HEC board members and founders. "He created an organization that brings in a tremendous amount of money, much, much faster than I ever thought it could. And the thing is, Jeff did that. He had to, because there's no other constant in that organization but him. The board members have come and gone.

Officers have come and gone. He's the one who has been there continuously, pushing, pushing, pushing."

Those who know Jeff well respond to those accomplishments with both nonchalant shoulder shrugs and wide-eyed amazement. The fact that he has been able to organize tens of thousands of environmental activists into an effective force surprises no one. "By nature, he's an absolute hell-raising type of grassroots activist," says Bill Hayden, an original HEC board member and a legislative lobbyist for HEC and other state environmental groups. "Jeff knows that it takes emotion to stir people up, and that's why he's good."

Tom Dustin: "His great strength was, and remains, in his forceful ability to organize legions around him, and to produce incredible public activism. He's one of the most exciting personalities in the Indiana environmental movement."

But creating and overseeing a million-dollar-a-year organization requires skills that Hayden and others weren't sure Jeff had when he was hired. "I don't think by nature he's an administrator," Hayden says. "But I think he's done an incredible job, a much better job than I thought he could. He has a vision. And it's got a long way to go before it is what he wants it to be."

Intense and *passionate* are two adjectives that inevitably come to mind when one thinks about Jeff. Both are expressed in the piercing focus that is apparent in his eyes when he talks about environmental issues. It's no wonder that the students at Greenwood repsonded when he shifted his emphasis from environmental career opportunities to the Hoosier National Forest. His passion is contagious.

"I think he really, really cares," Rothert says. "It's his value system and moral stance in terms of the environment over a long, long period of time, what we owe to future generations. He really believes that in a moral way, in an ethical way.

"I guess the thing that stands out about him most is that he's hung onto it. He started in the seventies when the wilderness fight was going on and on and on. A lot of people gave up. You get tired of hitting that brick wall. But he never gives up. He never gets to the point where he's ready to throw up his hands and go hibernate, which is what a lot of environmentalists do. There's not a lot of people still doing it. But Jeff's response is still the same as it was twenty years ago, which is amazing."

🕊 🕊 🕊 🕊

As HEC neared the end of its first decade in existence, Jeff found some time to sit down on a couple of occasions to reflect on the past and to contemplate the future.

At thirty-three, when we first sat down in his office in October 1992, Jeff says his view of the movement and reasons for being in it had evolved through the years. He smiles when talking about those traps that he sprang with youthful exuberance. In those days, he couldn't see hunters and trappers as anything but the enemy. Now it doesn't matter to him if hunters or trappers are standing next to him at a regulatory agency hearing, as long as they are on his side. His attitude toward them has tended to mellow. "I see the sportsmen constituency as being a major ally in questions about whether to build highways to nowhere and put theme parks on public lands and just keep making our whole economic development strategy simply a question of real-estate speculation and raising land prices," he now says. "I've sort of drifted away from the animal rights standpoint over the last ten years, even though my heart's still there. I'm much more into procedure and organizing and strategy than philosophy."

Jeff sees HEC and the movement itself as having made tremendous strides and gaining in effectiveness as they enter the final few years of the twentieth century. Environmentalists have moved beyond being nothing but reactionary naysayers trying to tear things down. They are finding ways to characterize the movement in a positive light by proposing what should be done. They are for energy efficiency, an auto industry that can compete with high-mileage cars from other countries, things that will improve American industry. And as a result, their credibility is growing.

One reason for that increasing effectiveness, and something that environmentalists should not forget, is the fundamental soundness of their message, he says. The movement's precepts are so logical, so basic, so easy for the human mind to comprehend, that they cannot be denied. It's a level of concern that's spontaneous in people. "There's nothing the media can do to stamp it out," he says. "There's nothing the politicians can do to stamp it out. And it will continue to grow. It's an unavoidable realization by humans that they love the planet and don't want to see it destroyed just for the sake of mindless growth and laissez-faire capitalism. I think that's why it grows. It's just so basic."

Jeff says there are some fundamental strategies that environmentalists must follow for the movement to continue increasing in power and influence.

First, they must focus their efforts more on the bigger political picture rather than on small, individual battles. "You need to be savvy enough to know that if you're not involved in the electoral process and you're not involved in the party platform process and you aren't building enough support to form your own third party, that you're cutting your own neck if you think the politicians are too slimy to get involved with," he charges. "It isn't their fault, it's your fault. You're just in it because you like to hear yourself talk a lot."

Second, they must stop trying to force an environmental ethic onto politicians. More and more they have to turn their focus toward educating the people and getting them to force the change on their elected officials. A greening of the state legislature and Congress is what he says is needed. It's a change that must come from the grassroots up and not from Congress mandating more environmental statutes. "Fundamentally, we've put the cart before the horse in forcing change down people's throats instead of approaching it from the standpoint of having people say, 'There's got to be change, damn it, Congress, go along.' That's what we've got to do. We've got to get back into the statehouses and Congress and turn them green."

Finally, the movement must focus more on single issues as it did in the national forest fight to maximize its influence. Ultimately it was the clout from that statewide pressure that transformed the governor into a staunch supporter of the Conservationist Alternative and convinced all of the state's congressional delegation to support at least looking at it, thus helping to break the Forest Service. But getting the diverse elements of the movement to coalesce behind one issue was difficult. "The waste groups and the groups in the northwestern part of the state gave us so much grief over the national forest thing that it wasn't funny," he says. "But we made them go along with it anyway."

To continue making gains, Jeff says that environmentalists still have major hills to climb. And many of them exist on the internal landscape of the movement itself.

One of the more difficult challenges is figuring out how to deal with environmentalists' propensity toward unbending, unrealistic idealism. They cannot be idealistic to the point that they fail to make progress because they won't compromise.

Jeff agrees that environmentalists need to be forceful and strident. But no movement can always have it all, and the environment is the ultimate loser when efforts at compromise fail. Activists need to learn that often they have to choose the lesser of the evils. "'That person is a jerk' is the way they feel about this person running for the Senate," he says. "But they forget that the person he's running against has a 20 percent voting score, opposes the ban on recyclables in landfills, and does whatever Chem Waste Management wants."

The key, he says, is knowing when to be strident and when to compromise. Too often individuals and groups are willing to compromise just to get an issue to go away. But at other times they refuse to compromise even though they haven't built a popular base of support for their position. "It's a balance," Jeff says. "You have to know when to compromise. You don't compromise when the issue is in its relative infancy. You compromise when you are in a powerful position so that you can get something for what you give. I just don't think that the art of compromise is something people are very good at."

At no time during his years as an environmentalist was Jeff's philosophy on compromise tested more than during the 1994 legislature. At its 1993 congress in December, HEC set as its number one priority increasing the funding levels for the Indiana Department of Environmental Management. A showdown between Governor Evan Bayh and the Republican-controlled Senate in the 1993 session had effectively left IDEM without money to run its waste and clean water programs. Bayh threatened to turn responsibility for those programs back over to the EPA unless money was raised in 1994.

HEC participated in a task force appointed by the governor, indeed took a leading role in it, sitting at the table with the Indiana Manufacturers Association, the state chamber of commerce, and many of the state's industrial leaders. A consultant hired by the state concluded that IDEM needed $30 million just to run basic programs. A compromise was reached just before the legislative session began, and Jeff and state environmental leaders felt that they were near their goal.

But no sooner had the session begun than it was announced that the governor would seek $18 million for the agency, significantly more than in years past but just a little more than half of what the consultant said was the minimum needed. Senate Republicans, who sponsored the IDEM legislation, began chipping away at the agency's enforcement authority through the legislative process.

Jeff and the rest of the state's environmental community concluded that there was little room for compromise on the issue. They told Bayh to make good on his threat to return the programs to the feds. Bayh balked. They went to the EPA in Chicago and made their case to Region 5 head Val Adamkus.

The result was universal condemnation of the group. IDEM commissioner Kathy Prosser said that HEC lost credibility, that as a group, environmentalists weren't comfortable "with the position of power they occupy." An IMA lobbyist likened their actions to "stomping off the playground angry, saying, 'I won't play with you anymore.'" State senator Vi Simpson, a Bloomington Democrat and a traditional HEC ally, publicly criticized the organization, calling the situation one of viewing the cup as half empty or half full. To Vi, half a cup was better than an empty cup.

To Jeff, it was a matter of principle, and not one to compromise on. Whether the cup was half empty or half full didn't matter. Doing the job of protecting Indiana's environment from industrial pollution required a cup and a half. And Bayh's caving in to the state's regulated community and backing off his threat to return the programs was simply unacceptable. "Our first loyalty is to good environmental protection," Jeff says. "He gave away their strongest bargaining chip."

While he publicly called the session the most trying to his tenure in office, Jeff responded to criticisms that HEC had lost ground: "We want to make sure that we fought the good fight, no matter how flattened we are on the road."

Learning the art of compromise is but one barrier to success that Jeff says environmentalists still must crack. Others can be just as daunting and as destructive as anything the opposition can dream up.

What Jeff sees as the movement's most serious flaw is the constant infighting between groups and individuals that causes them to lose sight of their common goals. Schisms within organizations have caused the loss of good people, which ultimately hurt the groups. "One of the things you find out in this movement is that you've got as much trouble from within it as you do from your opponents," he says. "In fact, the closest I've ever come to leaving this movement has never been over opponents and what they were doing. It's always been over colleagues and people I consider to be my friends. It's just a constant internal-strife situation."

In addition to the confrontation with the HEC board in 1986, Jeff nearly lost his job on two other occasions because of internal differences on how to run the organization. In 1989, the HEC board fired Jeff and rehired him a week later. In 1994, faced with dramatically declining revenues and the attendant stresses, the board stripped Jeff of his power, only to reinvest him three months later.

Jeff sees the constant proliferation of new groups not as a flowering of the movement but as an organizational disaster. It's a dilution of clout, a constant reinventing of the wheel, a duplication of resources that the movement needs to spend more wisely.

That is not to say that new groups aren't sometimes needed, he says. Established groups can become too entrenched or plagued by internal strife, and new groups are needed to carry on fights effectively. But the focus should be on forming a unified front that can carry more weight when the struggles go to the front line.

Another important tenet that groups and environmentalists should be cognizant of is the need for new leadership from time to time, Jeff says. People do, at some point, reach the point where they have to draw back and pace themselves and do less. A key is to always have new people who are sacrificing at incredible levels and pulling organizations forward. "The problem often is it's hard to relinquish the reins of control when you need to, to let the organization go forward," he says. "I'm not saying that's always the case with every leader of every organization. I don't believe in term limits. But I believe people burn out, and when that's total, they should leave. I do think a group will suffer and will tend to disintegrate and become very factional if they lose sight of the need to keep recruiting people and get them doing things."

For the activists of the future, Jeff has some simple advice. "I would just encourage them to be bold, as David Brower always says. And push that to figure out where they stand on things from a moral standpoint. That's my philosophy. If it doesn't stir you in your guts, you're not going to stick it out. And politics can't be something that it's chic to lambaste. Politics is the essence of our existence. The more people say, 'I'm not going to vote for the bastards,' the more they're causing the problem. So I'd say to get involved, be bold, figure out where you stand on the issues, and don't stand out of the process."

❀ ❀ ❀ ❀

BOB KLAWITTER

Bob Klawitter lives the life he preaches. And his preaching has played a key role in keeping large sections of southern Indiana natural and free from the designs of those who would alter forever the region's natural character for economic gain. For more than two decades, Bob and Kathy Klawitter have lived on an isolated plot of land in southwest Orange County without the benefit of utility-generated electricity, growing and raising the majority of their own food. Bob was an early member of Protect Our Woods in 1985 and played a key role in overturning U.S. Forest Service plans for ORV trails and clearcutting in the Hoosier National Forest. When Bob learned that state officials in 1988 had approved a plan to develop a giant theme park/resort on Tillery Hill on the shores of nearby Patoka Lake, he led Protect Our Woods beyond forest issues and into general environmental activity. He organized his neighbors and the state environmental community against the $80 million development that had as a key player Mutual of Omaha's Jim Fowler. While Tillery Hill is a project that could be revived at any time, Bob's leadership on the issue had left it lifeless by the mid-nineties. Bob, fifty-seven, and Kathy still live in the woods near Dubois with their son Sam.

Blocking an $80 Million Theme Park

🌸 🌸 🌸 🌸 **6** When Bob Klawitter left the first public hearing on Tillery Hill back in May 1989, he was convinced that all was lost. The odds against stopping the megadevelopment on Patoka Lake just seemed overwhelming.

The proposal for an $80 million recreation complex on the Tillery Hill peninsula had been approved by the Indiana Natural Resources Commission in December 1988, subject to changes "to avoid any adverse environmental impacts foreseen in the environmental assessment." It was being pushed by a consortium of developers headed by William Reynolds, president of the Reynolds National Corporation and one of the wealthiest and most powerful men in southern Indiana.

The developers were selling the project—a resort hotel, a conference center, an amphitheater, forty-five villas, two golf courses, a marina, a pioneer theme park, thrill rides, shops, and a wild animal zoo to be developed by Jim Fowler, Marlin Perkins's animal handler on "Mutual of Omaha's Wild Kingdom"—as the shot in the arm the economically depressed area desperately needed. "Tillery Hill will help all of southern Indiana—Evansville, Boonville, the entire area," Reynolds had told the press in March 1988.

Such arguments were welcomed by those struggling to survive in one of the most economically depressed areas in the state. At the time, Orange County's unemployment rate was hovering around 7 percent, when the statewide average was about 4.

Reynolds's development group, called Patoka Partners Inc., was projecting that Tillery Hill would produce between 500 and 1,500 full- and part-time jobs and draw 1.5 million visitors a year to the region. A group of county leaders called Orange County 2000 had commissioned a feasibility study on the project by a Florida-based research firm that had done work on Disney World, Six Flags, and other recreational facilities.

More of Reynolds's comments in March 1988 illustrated the grandiose nature of the project that Bob and other environmentalists had decided to fight. For it to work, southern Indiana's highway system would need to be dramatically upgraded, Reynolds said. "If we are going to get investors to put $70 million plus in Tillery Hill, the roads will have to be a part of that. I think a four-lane Indiana 37 is crucial to the project. We would like to see that, and also a direct route from Indianapolis to Evansville."

The Partners' proposal was embraced by the area's leading citizens. "I think it'll add to our economy," Paoli Chamber of Commerce president Mabel Fultz was quoted as saying. "Also, it will be a clean industry." Orange County commissioner and businessman Rex Babcock summed up the faith locals had in the Patoka Partners: "Hell, anything in life is a gamble. The group of people involved in this is just a high caliber of people. And if they go out and spend 70 million on this, they know what they're doing, or they wouldn't spend so much money."

By the time the first public hearing on the environmental-impact statement rolled around a little more than a year later, the Patoka Partners also had the support of the Indiana Department of Natural Resources, the lieutenant governor, and, apparently, the community. More than two hundred people attended the hearing in French Lick. And most applauded when Orange County commissioner Amos Dorsam said that Tillery Hill would bring with it improved roads, industry, and jobs. Dorsam scoffed at claims that it would cause environmental damage and said the opposition stemmed mainly from newcomers to the area and outsiders.

Of the twenty-four who spoke about the project that night, only ten were against it. And they did include several newcomers and outsiders—Bob and Kathy Klawitter and Andy Mahler from Protect Our Woods, Jeff Foster from the Sierra Club, and both Jeff Stant and Jeff St. Clair from the Hoosier Environmental Council. Bob, clad in his characteristic wool plaid coat and muddy work boots, had given an eloquent speech about how wonderful it was to live in southern Indiana and raise children, and how the hordes of people that would be attracted to Tillery Hill would change it all, for the worse. Mahler said that the jobs would be low-paying and seasonal. Stant had looked and sounded impressive in his coat and tie, passionately arguing that the project would be an environmental disaster. But he was an environmentalist from Indianapolis and not likely to have much influence with the locals. One of the local opponents, Marian Barclay, waffled a bit, saying she hadn't realized the development was going to have educational aspects. And Kathy, who waited until the last minute to speak, was necessarily reserved in her presentation. The superintendent of the small school system she teaches in was among those who spoke for the project.

Bob says that it all just seemed too much to overcome. "We came back, and Jeff and Kathy and I got drunk that night. We figured we had lost right at that first hearing."

Bob Klawitter was indeed an outsider to the Orange County community. A native of Gary, he had been an English professor at Indiana University in Bloomington in the 1960s. His involvement in the antiwar politics of the time led to a short-lived career in academia. He had served as literary editor of the Spectator, a radical underground campus newspaper, and had taught a creative writing class that engaged in guerrilla theater and did "some pretty heavy actions on the university campus." Such activities, Bob knew, would not be tolerated by IU officials. But he also knew that it would have been too controversial for them to fire him during the student movement. "So they waited until a couple of years later and my tenure decision came up, and they didn't give it to me. I left without a fuss. I was ready to go. I didn't want to work for them anymore, anyway."

Bob participated in the original Earth Day in 1970 and saw that one era—that of the antiwar and civil rights movements that he had been so involved in—was giving way to another, that of the environmental movement. But he had grown weary of activism and decided to look to Thoreau rather than Emerson for inspiration. He decided not to talk about the new movement or organize people to participate in it. He decided to live it. "This was our environmental project," he says, sweeping his hand in a circular motion, pointing to the valley he calls home. "Come down here and live off the grid and not have any utilities, and raise most of our own food and build our own house and live sustainably. You could say that the first thing that I did was to move down here and give up society."

"Down here" is an eighty-acre plot of land in the southwestern corner of Orange County on the Dubois County line. Bob had a small pension from the university and some savings from his salary that he and Kathy, one of his former students, used to buy the land. "If we'd have had $100,000 we could have bought the whole watershed," he says. But not only did they not have $100,000, there wasn't any money at all in Bob's vision of the future. He had decided to live without money, opting for a life of labor and barter, gardening, helping neighbors put up hay, doing spring plowing, taking care of cattle, working with a local man doing veterinary work, and butchering livestock in exchange for what he and Kathy would need to live. His life plan, however, was a little too much for Kathy. "We were real poor," he says. "We had to think when we left home if we had enough money to get to town and buy enough gas to get home and back to town again. She thought that my lifestyle was abject poverty, and she didn't want any part of that."

Kathy suggested an alternative arrangement, to which Bob agreed. She would provide the money by teaching in the nearby Dubois school system. And they lived quite comfortably under that arrangement until the day in 1985 when friends Andy Mahler and Linda Lee came by seeking their support in the fight for the Hoosier National Forest. Bob offered to do an economic-impact analysis of the Forest Service's plans. "That was the end of sustainable living," Kathy says. "That was the end of gardening. We had to have a computer and cars that were much more reliable." But their dedication to principle convinced them that the tradeoff was worth it. "We were very reluctant to give up our isolation, which was very luxuriant," Bob says. "But we felt like, if you believe these things, you've got to do something about it. So we did."

Bob had been involved in environmental activities for only a couple of years when he stood up to speak against Tillery Hill that May 1989 evening in French Lick. But losing wasn't something he was used to. He had been one of the early members of Protect Our Woods, an environmental group formed to fight a proposed management plan that would have allowed off-road vehicles and clearcutting in the Hoosier National Forest. And he had played a central role in winning that battle.

With no background in forestry whatsoever, Bob had analyzed a box full of raw computer data generated by U.S. Forest Service scientists on Indiana's timber inventory and had made a persuasive case that there was no need to log in the Hoosier at all. There was enough timber on private lands. Ending below-cost public timber sales would increase the value of private timber and put more money in local people's pockets. The more private timberland became profitable, the less incentive there would be to convert it to other uses. Bob set out to prove that ending logging in the national forest would help his neighbors who own timber and work in the wood industry, not hurt them. And this question, in one form or another, has been central to his thinking ever since. It leads to the philosophical principle he considers his most important contribution to Indiana's environmental movement: Environmental degradation causes economic decline.

A pivotal point in the Hoosier fight came during a negotiation session set up by the Forest Service when the timber industry's leading negotiator looked across the table at Bob and said, "Klawitter, you're too smart for your own good. Someday you're going to outsmart yourself." The timber industry then walked away from the negotiations, and an environmentalist proposal for forest management was ultimately adopted by the Forest Service.

Bob's second foray into environmental activism came when a cabinetmaker friend from Crawford County told him of plans by a Cincinnati company to build a giant sawmill in the region that would have put local mill owners out of business. Government officials were lined up to give the company tax breaks and other incentives to develop the "economically depressed" land it wanted. After researching the matter, Bob learned that the property in question was actually productive farmland. He got a lawyer. The project was scrapped.

Tillery Hill, however, seemed another matter. Or at least it did the night of the French Lick public hearing.

Patoka Lake is a serene, 8,900-acres lake that sprawls lazily through the southern Indiana counties of Orange, Crawford, and Dubois. Indiana's second-largest body of water, it was created by the U.S. Army Corps of Engineers as part of a program to control flooding in the Ohio River Valley. Between 1938 and 1988, the corps built seventy-eight dams along Ohio River tributaries, including the one on the Patoka River that formed Patoka Lake. The corps owns the lake and leases the shoreline to the Indiana Department of Natural Resources, which is responsible for its management. All DNR activities on Patoka must ultimately be approved by the corps.

In 1976, the DNR created a master plan for managing Patoka Lake that called for a state recreation area on the 1,779-acre Tillery Hill peninsula. The plan designated the peninsula for commercial development, similar to the Fairfax complex at Lake Monroe near Bloomington. It called for the DNR to lease Tillery Hill to private developers, who would build a lodge, marina, and other recreational facilities on it. The DNR would operate three other, undeveloped recreation areas on the lake under the master plan.

No developers were found willing to undertake the project until the mid-1980s, when Patoka Partners put forward their proposal. The Partners consisted of Reynolds and his wife, Sharon; Dugan and Meyers Construction of Cincinnati; Bill and Sharon Rouse, former owners of the Cedar Point amusement park near Sandusky, Ohio; and "Wild Kingdom" star Fowler.

But despite the enthusiasm with which local movers and shakers greeted the Partners' plan, it had some weaknesses. First, it was far larger than what was called for in the DNR's master plan. And because it had taken so long to get a development plan in place, the DNR had opened the peninsula to hunting and other forms of dispersed recreation. Hunters, one of the DNR's prime constituencies, had come to view the peninsula as their own and saw development on it as taking something away from them.

And then there was the decision to locate the project within a mile of Bob Klawitter's cabin in the rugged Orange County woods. That made the fight close to Bob's heart, and he took his case to an initially reluctant Protect Our Woods board. "I proposed that we pick up the fight against Tillery Hill because that's my neighborhood," Bob says. "It was more important to me than the national forest. But Protect Our Woods didn't want to do it. There were a lot of people who felt we ought to stay with the national forest issue exclusively and expand that struggle. And they also thought we couldn't win Tillery Hill. Eighty million dollars, how can we beat that? That's incredible. Well, my point of view was, I've got to fight this. If you guys don't want to fight it with me, I'll have to start another organization and fight it myself. So they said, 'OK, let's fight it. Basically, you do it.' And we've been incredibly successful."

The phrase "incredibly successful" is not at all an overstatement, considering what happened in the fight·against Tillery Hill. With Bob Klawitter leading the way, environmentalists stopped the Patoka Partners and their supporters in the upper echelons of the DNR and the corps dead in their tracks. Tillery Hill is unlikely ever to be built.

⚜ ⚜ ⚜ ⚜

Bob knew from the time he first took up the fight against Tillery Hill, a year and a half or so before the first public hearing, that it would be an uphill battle. And he attacked it in typical Klawitter fashion, with what Kathy calls the focus of a "disciplined scholar." He mapped out a three-pronged approach. He figured local people needed to be convinced that they had something to lose, the environmental movement statewide had to be convinced that it was an issue worth fighting for, and the project had to be fought on legal grounds at the administrative level.

One lesson that Bob had learned from the early days of the fight over the national forest was the importance of establishing local support for environmental fights. So, sharpest among the three prongs of his Tillery Hill strategy was rallying locals to the cause. There were two main obstacles to convincing local people that Tillery Hill was not in their best interests. First was the argument that it would somehow improve their lives by bringing money into the community. Second was their doubts that the powers that be could be stopped.

Bob focused on the message that while there might be more money coming into the region, it would carry a price. "'Nobody gives you anything for nothing,'" he says that he would tell anyone who would listen. "'They're buying something from you, and what they're buying from you is this natural, fairly uncrowded, peaceful, crime-free environment where you like to live and bring up your kids. You want to sell that to bring Tillery Hill here? That's what you're doing. You're bringing in crime, you're bringing in drugs, you're bringing in traffic, you're bringing in people, you're bringing in pollution. You're going to destroy your water supply.' That was a big argument. Tillery Hill is in the middle of their water supply. And everybody remembers how bad the water supply was around here."

Bob says that he knew he was having an effect when people would come up to him at his son's Little League games and tell him to keep it up. There were people who were opposed to Tillery Hill but didn't really know how much until they heard someone else talk about it. "When they saw somebody stand up and fight it and look credible, then they began to think they had some hope. The sentiment was out there, and we just sort of stood up and became a lightning rod for it. And that's all it took, really, it turns out."

Aside from focusing on quality of life, Bob hit hard on the effect Tillery Hill would have on the lake. Patoka Lake provides drinking water to five counties, and he pointed out that there is no other place in the area where a reservoir could be built. Estimates that lakes such as Monroe and Patoka would have useful lives of two hundred years have already been cut. The more the lake watershed is developed, the faster it will silt up and become unusable, Bob argued. He also worked on the sportsmen who used the peninsula for hunting and the lake for fishing and boating. Hunters would lose a prime hunting ground, he pointed out. And fishermen and boaters would find an already crowded lake even more crowded if 1.5 million visitors were drawn by Tillery Hill each year.

While Bob knew that developing local support for the fight was critical to any chance of success, he also knew that it was going to take more than just local opposition to defeat the powerful pro–Tillery Hill forces. It was going to take statewide pressure from the environmental movement as well, and he needed a strategy to bring that pressure to bear on the DNR. He joined the Hoosier Environmental Council and started serving on its board. "I realized that we couldn't beat this by ourselves. We needed help. And in order to get this help, we had to help other people with their projects. This wider network was crucial to us. So I got connected to HEC real thoroughly."

Bob thought he had the perfect vehicle for galvanizing statewide opposition to Tillery Hill in the involvement of Jim Fowler. Here was a guy who was perceived as an environmentalist and was doing radio spots nationwide, including the local Paoli radio station, about wildlife and conservation for the National Wildlife Federation. Yet he was involved in a project that Bob considered an environmental travesty.

Bob took on Fowler on two fronts. First, he wrote to Jay Hair, director of the National Wildlife Federation, and told him that the project threatened bald eagle habitat. Others also wrote to complain about Fowler and about the pro-exploitation policies of NWF's Indiana affiliate. The NWF sent a team to Indiana to unsuccessfully try and reconcile the different points of view. The other tack was to write a letter to Fowler and publicize it around the state. Bob sent it to key people in the state environmental movement and government and published a copy in the February 1989 HEC *Monitor,* the environmental council's monthly publication, in which members and groups express their views. In it he took Fowler to task for participating in a project that seemed to be contrary to his professed values.

"Jim, this is the urban sprawl that you say you detest so much," he wrote. "1,800 acres of wildlife habitat will be destroyed in a state which has very little wild land left. Some of Indiana's most promising eagle nesting habitat will be destroyed." He went on to list other species that would have been adversely affected by the development—the swamp rabbit, small mammals, reptiles, amphibians, birds, timber rattlesnakes, copperheads, cottonmouth moccasins. "I don't need to tell you how the destruction of these wild populations will eventually endanger the human species. Jim, we live in a relatively undeveloped countryside surrounded by the Indianapolis, Evansville, Louisville, and Cincinnati metropolitan areas. These cities threaten to stretch out and overwhelm us. Managers of our state and federal lands are promoting the developed recreation sites and highways that will finish us off. Tillery Hill and its highway will be a stake through the heart of our rural community."

Fowler spoke with Bob when both were in Indianapolis for a Natural Resources Commission hearing on Tillery Hill. Fowler said he had been assured that no endangered species would be affected by the park and his wild animal zoo. "I said, 'Yeah, they aren't endangered yet.' What he wanted to do was have this zoo here so that African species could be appreciated. However, that was displacing all the indigenous species. We talked about that. It's hard to know whether that had any impact. I doubt it. But it seems like pressure over the long haul had, because other people said that too." Basically, Fowler ducked the entire issue. He has never spoken with the media about it or made any public statements. But that wasn't the point, Bob says. He wasn't trying to change Fowler's mind with the letter. He was trying to reach the statewide environmental movement.

The Fowler letter attracted the attention of Dan Carpenter, who wrote several pieces on Tillery Hill in his *Indianapolis Star* column. Carpenter also brought the Klawitters together with Indianapolis Channel 20's Mike Atwood, who was shooting a documentary on Patoka Lake. The Klawitters and their point of view figured prominently in Atwood's hour-long "Patoka: Lake of Memories, River of Dreams," which was broadcast several times. One of the people the video helped to convince was Kathy's school superintendent, who played it at a school board meeting. Taking the message to the state arena ended up bringing it home to the local community.

Bob and the Tillery Hill opponents also used the system against the developers and the DNR. HEC's St. Clair and the Sierra Club's Foster in January 1989 wrote an administrative appeal of the project. Among the issues raised were that the project was significantly larger than anything called for in the DNR's master plan for Tillery Hill, and that the Corps of Engineers had not done an environmental-impact statement on it as required by federal law. The Corp of Engineers and the DNR agreed in March that indeed a full-blown EIS was required for Tillery Hill. With that decision came the requirement for a public hearing, the May 16 French Lick hearing, after which Bob had thought all was lost.

But disillusionment over Tillery Hill quickly gave way to hope. On his way back to Indianapolis the morning after the French Lick hearing, Jeff Stant stopped at a gas station in Paoli to call and tell Bob the news. Local radio news accounts of the public hearing were focusing on the fact that there was opposition to Tillery Hill, playing excerpts from Bob's speech. "Jeff called and said, 'Maybe there's a chance here after all,'" Bob says.

※ ※ ※ ※

Three days after the hearing, on May 19, the Indiana attorney general's office proposed an "Agreed Order" under which both the HEC appeal and the project would be put on hold pending completion of an EIS. Opponents of Tillery Hill had new life. The tide had taken a sudden and unexpected turn. Bob took advantage of the new momentum, continuing to pursue his three-prong strategy.

As work was progressing on the EIS, Bob and the project's opponents gained some valuable support from the U.S. Fish and Wildlife Service office in Bloomington. F&W director Dave Hudak wrote a four-page letter to the corps in October 1989, raising concerns about the project's potential impact on efforts to reintroduce nesting bald eagles in southern Indiana. Patoka Lake and Tillery Hill are among the best potential eagle nesting locales in the state, he wrote. "Alternatives with less environmental impacts should be carefully studied. We feel a lodge and cabins with a network of trails would have much less environmental impact and be more in line with the current uses of Patoka Reservoir properties."

Tillery Hill proponents reluctantly acquiesced to Hudak's request. "Because of the scrutiny this project has been getting from environmental groups, we didn't want to look lax," Bob Woodyard, chief of the corps' Louisville office, said in December. "The bottom line is, we're going to undertake those studies." The studies caused a several-month delay in completion of the EIS, giving Bob and environmentalists time to continue making their case.

The seventy-one-page draft EIS was finally released in February 1991. It said the project's environmental impact would be minimal. Some silt, fertilizers, pesticides, and herbicides would find their way to the water. Most of the negative impact would be on the peninsula's wildlife—coyote, fox, grouse, quail, wild turkey, and some songbirds. "Development at Tillery Hill would cause some disturbance of wintering eagles" and "would reduce the probability of bald eagles nesting successfully at Patoka Lake," the EIS concluded.

Procedure called for the corps to receive public comment on the statement, make any necessary revisions, and then prepare a final EIS. The final statement would have a number of alternatives from which the corps would ultimately choose, ranging from doing nothing to intense development. At that time, Woodyard indicated that the Partners' proposal was the most likely choice. "I'd say there's better than a fifty-fifty chance that it will be approved as proposed. We might stipulate some limitations to construction techniques and parameters, or require some types of buffer zones between the wildlife habitats, for example."

As part of the public comment process, the corps scheduled a March 26, 1991, public hearing in Jasper. It became a showcase for the work that Bob and the environmental community had done on Tillery Hill. More than three hundred people attended, and only a handful supported the project. They sang the same old economic-development song. "This is an opportunity to pull ourselves out of this economic rut," Jerry Ihrig, owner of the Patoka Chalets south of Paoli, said at the hearing. John Duncan, owner of the Patoka Lake Village resort cabins, added: "They say public lands belong to the public. But how much of the public would be able to use that land if we don't allow this development?"

More argued the arguments Bob Klawitter and environmentalists had been making. "You can't pour concrete without permanently negatively impacting the environment," said Steve Knox of the Indiana Sport Anglers Alliance, pointing out that the lake is shallow and could easily be silted by runoff from Tillery Hill. He also spoke of money matters: "Public lands should not be used by private promoters to line their personal pockets with profits." Patoka neighbor Bill Edwards asked: "Who's going to pay to fix the roads and dispose of the trash from all these visitors?"

"We had everybody lined up against it," Bob says. "The Bass Federation was there opposed to it. The Dubois County sportsmen were against it. Local landowners and farmers spoke against it. And vets, Vietnam vets, were against it. One guy got up and said, 'I went over there and fought in Vietnam for four years. I was always dreaming of coming back to southern Indiana. But it wasn't Disneyland I was dreaming of coming back to.'" Written comments against the project also poured in to the Corps of Engineers.

Ever the disciplined scholar, Bob also dissected the EIS line by line. He found it lacking in several respects and sent his analysis to the U.S. Environmental Protection Agency in Chicago, whose approval on the EIS was needed before the project could move forward. "It was a mess. It was very vulnerable," Bob says. His analysis showed that the Tillery Hill development would damage the region's water quality and the area's biological resources without providing the economic benefits claimed by the developers.

In July 1991, word started leaking out that the EPA had reached the same conclusion. In early August, DNR deputy director Jack Costello acknowledged that the EPA had found "inadequacies" in the EIS. The agency had identified six environmental areas in which it said the EIS was lacking sufficient information: water quality and erosion control; secondary economic and land-use impacts; effects on wildlife habitat; impacts on air, noise, and infrastructure such as roads, sewage, landfills, and water supply; details on the exotic animal park; and details on the theme park.

Costello declined to pronounce the project dead. "Nothing's really stopped," he said. "We're just looking at shoring up what appear to be inadequacies in the environmental impact statement." The DNR told the developers they would have to provide the information. The Patoka Partners said they would. They didn't. And without that information, the EIS cannot be completed and Tillery Hill will remain rugged and undeveloped, just the way Bob Klawitter wants it.

At times it has seemed that luck has played an important role in Bob's success. When the nearby town of Huntingburg, which relies on Patoka Lake for its water, developed serious water supply problems amid the controversy over Tillery Hill, a reporter from Jasper told Bob and Kathy that it appeared that God was on their side. Such a perception was reinforced in the spring of 1992 when a pair of bald eagles nested right on the Tillery Hill peninsula.

But those who know and have worked with Bob Klawitter know that good fortune has little to do with his success. It's his intelligence, dedication, and personality that have catapulted him into the role of one of the most powerful environmental forces in the state.

The Izaak Walton League's Tom Dustin: "Bob—and we must include his wife Kathy—is perhaps the most articulate forest-protection advocate I know. No one anywhere does the level of homework that he does in demonstrating that there is little if any need for timbering on the public forests. It is not possible to win a debate on this subject, or on most any other subject, with Bob Klawitter. While some of us know our issues very well, no one cuts through to the core questions as well as Bob does. Yet, Bob is invariably pleasant and respectful. A mirthful sense of humor adds to this facility, as well as a calm, intellectual approach."

Veteran environmental activist and lobbyist Bill Hayden: "He's brilliant. And he has a great deal of respect and value for rural culture. He thinks that those 'hillbillies' down there aren't all that dumb. And I don't think he's wrong on that. He has an ecological vision that I don't always understand. And he also has a very strong commitment to property rights."

Alison Cochran, who has worked with Bob since Protect Our Woods was formed in the mid-1980s, stresses that Bob's commitment to environmentalism extends beyond his focus on public policy. Like Andy Mahler and Linda Lee, Bob and Kathy, whose rustic cabin is powered by solar energy, have incorporated their environmental ethic completely into their everyday lives. "By their choice to live in the woods, they have integrated their beliefs into their lifestyle to a large extent. Going to their houses is like going to another world. You realize that when you're there and you very quickly become a part of it."

While many successful activists rely on their abilities to organize others, Bob, while he has that ability as well, is more accurately described as an individual dynamo who inspires others with his tremendous reserve of intelligence and energy. "I've learned so much, and continue to, every time I've talked to Bob," Alison Cochran says. "His dedication, his single-mindedness, I admire them. But it can be difficult from time to time. He's a challenging person to be with. His intellect demands respect, and part of the respect is paying close enough attention, having done your homework, so that you are ready to listen to him and can make use of what he's talking about. But my first impression of Bob was how gentle he was. He's very kind and open."

Bob Klawitter does not appear at first glance to be the type of person who could overcome such daunting odds and prevail. He is an ample man of average height, whose face and features, while somewhat weathered, belie his age, fifty-seven. He looks perhaps ten years younger. And he just doesn't seem to take things too seriously. When he is talking about the most serious of subjects, his conversation is frequently punctuated with laughter. Sitting on a panel of experts, testifying before an Indiana Senate committee on some environmental issue, or striding to the microphone at a public hearing in his secondhand clothes, he seems out of place.

But one need only listen to Bob speak for a while to realize he is not an "idiot with an outhouse," as he sometimes describes himself, that his friends' impressions are on target, that he is an environmental philosopher of considerable influence. He puts the Tillery hill controversy into a historical perspective that few who have been intimately involved with it have ever even considered.

"We've been through all of this once in southern Indiana," he says, referring to the wave of settlement the region barely survived in the mid- to late 1800s. "All the people moved in, they saw all of what looked like rich land that grew big trees. They cut down all the trees, started farming the hillsides. All the soil washed down the hillsides and it was gone, and they had to move elsewhere and abandon this part of the world. The forest grew back up, and now they see it as the last frontier for development again. They've built the dams to provide the water supply that never existed here. Hey, they can come in and see all this natural beauty, and they can build houses amongst it. Until the water supply gives out and the biological system collapses and then we're back to another abandonment. Well, why not foresee that? It's better to build down than to crash."

Bob also puts the situation into a broader perspective of natural history to explain why the region can never be sustainably developed. "The basic thing is that this place is karst topography. This escarpment over here, the Crawford Upland, is developing karst. Our spring is dissolved out of the limestone and comes out over the shale ledge where we get our drinking water. This is just like the Mitchell Plain over by Orleans, only it's a few thousand years down the road. But it's dissolving away. This is not glaciated. There's no soil here. It is very thin. And the result is that there is no water here. The water all runs away through these underground passages. There's no lakes. The rivers are shallow. And the second thing is that it floods. As soon as the underground channels fill up in heavy rains, they flood. Most of this whole area is a flood plain, except for the ridges. We all live on the flood plain.

"So you've got too much water and not enough water, all at the same time. Alternately, you don't have enough, and then you have too much. And all the attempts they make to change that are going to fail. It's hydrologically impossible short of re-engineering the planet. This place is a sieve with limited capacity. There's no way they can develop this place sustainably. The reason this region has got a forest left in it is because it's undevelopable. These are natural impossibilities that they can overcome briefly, very briefly. They can spend a lot of money and temporarily overcome these things. And then it will all go away, and they will have destroyed what's here naturally, and they'll have lost all this money. Well, that doesn't help society in any way."

Bob speaks equally as eloquently on why environmentalists have been so successful in staving off Tillery Hill. "Just because you are outnumbered, you don't give up. If you're right, if you've got the good analysis, if your analysis fits the facts, you've got them beat right there. The truth is, they don't have the facts down very well because they haven't been looking for the facts. They've been looking for rationales for what they're doing.

"These people have no idea what to do with themselves. They don't understand that there's anything else you can do except make money. See, we're fighting for our neighborhood, the life of our neighborhood. It just isn't comparable with what they're into. Basically, they don't care as much. We care enough to devote our lives to fighting them. They don't care enough to devote their lives to fighting us. That's part of it. We care more than they do."

❧ ❧ ❧ ❧

JOHN FOSTER

John Foster was well into his second decade of fighting for a safe cleanup of PCB contamination in Bloomington when he sat down to talk about his career as an environmentalist in 1994. For twelve years John had been an integral part of a core group of environmental activists that had taken on the Westinghouse Electric Corporation and city, state, and federal officials who wanted to build an experimental trash-fueled hazardous-waste incinerator in Bloomington. He was a founding member of the Monroe County Environmental Coalition and worked with numerous other groups and individuals who eventually turned public opinion so irretrievably against the incinerator that the plan was abandoned nine years after it was proposed. Trained as an artist, John has worked a variety of jobs throughout his life, including as a civil engineer and mechanic for energy and construction companies, a researcher for a Bloomington lawyer who specialized in environmental litigation, the manager of a print shop, and a car salesman. John, fifty-two, lives in rural Monroe County with his wife, Deidre. He has three grown children of his own and two grown stepchildren.

Killing an Incineration Experiment

7 When John Foster was working on an emergency Superfund cleanup in Bloomington back in 1982, he had no idea of the cataclysmic changes his life was about to undergo.

❀ ❀ ❀ ❀

He was working for a local contractor that had received an EPA contract to remediate an old landfill at Bennett's Quarry near Bloomington, where PCB-contaminated electrical capacitors from the nearby Westinghouse plant had been dumped years before. Westinghouse had produced capacitors, which used PCBs as an insulating fluid, at the plant between 1957 and 1978. Until 1971, PCB-laden wastes and defective capacitors were routinely discarded in the company's trash and taken to various public and private dumps in and around Bloomington.

John was heading a crew that, as he puts it, was excavating a hillside and moving dirt down to cover the contaminated area. He viewed the project as just another job. He didn't believe that he or his workers were at any risk at the Bennett's Quarry dump. "I had heard both sides, that PCBs hurt you and that PCBs don't hurt you," he says. "I believed the state of Indiana. I didn't believe there was anything harmful about PCBs or capacitors."

That's not to say that John was comfortable with the way the cleanup was being handled. In fact, he often found himself scratching his head in bemusement at the way the EPA was directing the project. He pointed out to EPA officials overseeing the project that there was a spring running through the site. They asked him if there was a way to contain the water flow. John said he could try, but he couldn't guarantee anything. EPA officials told him just to do his best and went back to Chicago, leaving John to his own devices.

Then the crew started to erect a security fence around the dump area. But each time they would drill fence holes, they would hit capacitors. They would move the fence line out a few feet, and the same thing would happen. Finally, after four or five such attempts, John contacted EPA officials. They told him to put the fence up at the original location and not to worry about it.

When it came time to cover the capped dump, the topsoil used had Johnson grass in it. John says that Johnson grass is a tuber that actually penetrates clay, dies, and leaves holes where it had grown. That would allow water to penetrate the clay cap, which, it seemed to him, defeated the purpose of capping the landfill to begin with. EPA knew about the problem and did nothing.

"Having never worked around EPA, I didn't know what the norm was," John says. "So I just assumed that I had a couple of guys here who had good intentions but didn't have any idea what they were doing. I also assumed that when EPA said they were going to send someone back and take care of the rest of the problem, they would do that. I just wrote it off to this is the way Westinghouse and EPA have agreed to do this."

John didn't think much about the problems at the quarry dump until his company got another contract a few months later to do a remedial cleanup at two other old PCB dumps—Neal's Landfill west of Bloomington and Neal's Dump in Owen County near Spencer. Again, much of what happened there didn't seem right. For example, the crew was supposed to remove "surface capacitors" from the site. But for each layer of capacitors they dug up, they exposed additional layers. After EPA officials debated the issue for months, they decided that most of what the crew had dug up didn't meet the definition of surface capacitors and had the crew rebury them.

"I mean, why, once you have excavated something you know to be hazardous that you're going to have to get rid of sooner or later, would you bury it again?" John asks. "Once again I just blew this off as Westinghouse and EPA working together. But it had become real obvious that nobody out there had any idea what was going on."

Even though John felt that the cleanup itself was a farce, he still had some faith in the powers that were overseeing the project. When some of his workers began questioning whether they were being exposed to harmful chemicals, John assured them that they weren't. Officials from the State Board of Health had been on the sites several times. "If they weren't wearing white suits and respirators, then we don't need to," he says he told the workers. The workers' questions were ones that John took personally. Not only was he on site day after day, but so was his youngest son, whom he had hired on the crew.

John basically looked upon the entire cleanup fiasco with detached cynicism until the summer of 1984, when Mayor Tomi Allison announced that an agreement had been reached with Westinghouse to clean up several contaminated areas in and around Bloomington. He made an appointment with the mayor, telling her his story about the emergency cleanups, saying that he didn't know where else to turn. The mayor blew him off. "What I found out was that I had opened a big can of worms that nobody was supposed to get into," John says.

John's frustration turned to outright anger later that year when he read an old letter from the State Board of Health that said no one working at Neal's Landfill should be there without respirators and full-body covering.

At that point, John's life took an irreversible turn toward environmental activism. He became a dedicated opponent of the proposed PCB cleanup agreement. "The combination of Tomi not listening to me and the state lying to me just ticked me off so much that as long as I could see that things were headed the wrong way, I was going to stay involved."

Ten years later, John Foster was still fighting for a safe and reasonable cleanup of Bloomington's PCB contamination.

PCBs (polychlorinated biphenyls) are manmade chemicals that, because of their physical characteristics, have been used widely in the United States since the late 1920s in a variety of commercial applications. Because of their high stability, low volatility, and nonflammability, PCBs were ideal chemicals for use as insulating fluids in electrical capacitors and transformers, significantly improving efficiency and fire safety. It's estimated that 70 percent of the PCBs manufactured in the United States were used in such electrical equipment. To a lesser degree, they were used in hydraulic fluids, heat transfer fluids, lubricants, plasticizers, paints, and primers, as well as in degreasers, casting waxes, inks, and carbonless copying paper, and as silo liners.

Chemically, PCBs are molecules composed of three chemical elements: hydrogen, carbon, and chlorine. When heated, PCBs can produce by-products of polychlorinated dibenzofurans and polychlorinated dibenzo-p-dioxins. Furans have the same chemical makeup as PCBs but with an additional oxygen molecule, while dioxins have two additional oxygen molecules. Dioxins, which are among the most toxic chemicals in existence, were the active ingredients in Agent Orange, the deadly defoliant used in Vietnam. All PCBs manufactured in the United States between 1929 and 1978 were manufactured by the Monsanto Corporation.

The same properties that made PCBs ideal for industrial use—their extreme stability and nonsolubility in water—also made them persistent environmental pollutants. And because they are soluble in fatty tissues in animals, PCBs tend to accumulate and concentrate in the food chain.

The body of scientific knowledge about the health effects of PCBs has been developing for the past fifty-plus years, almost as long as they have been in use. Seven years after PCBs were first manufactured and marketed by Monsanto, Dr. Louis Schwartz wrote in two medical journals in 1936 about the possible adverse health effects that could result from workers' exposure to the chemicals. "In addition to . . . skin lesions, symptoms of systemic poisoning have occurred among workers inhaling these fumes," he wrote in the June 1936 edition of the *American Journal of Public Health.* "Those working with [PCBs] have complained of digestive disturbance, burning of the eyes, impotence and hematuria." Three months later, Schwartz wrote in the *Public Health Bulletin,* "Workers . . . should be periodically examined for symptoms of systematic poisoning."

Because of their physical characteristics, their widespread use, and mounting evidence that PCBs were a health hazard, Congress in 1976 passed the Toxic Substances Control Act (TSCA), which banned the manufacture of PCBs after January 1, 1979, and banned their distribution in commerce after July 1, 1979, unless specifically exempted by the administrator of the EPA.

❧ ❧ ❧ ❧

PCBs are one of the most widely dispersed toxic chemicals on the planet. Traces of them have been detected in the most remote reaches of Earth. But there are no definitive studies on the effects of PCBs on the general population.

Between the late 1970s, when the manufacture of PCBs was banned, and the 1990s, studies showed that PCB concentrations in animal tissues declined. Studies of atmospheric levels produced inconsistent results. Curious about those inconsistencies, Indiana University professor and environmental chemist Ronald Hites revisited the topic in a study released in 1994.

Hites and a graduate student collected air samples in Bloomington and in Bermuda to test for the presence of PCBs. They found that atmospheric concentrations had remained constant. They also found PCB concentrations in Bloomington to be three times greater than in Bermuda and about 40 percent higher than other studies had shown in the air over Lake Superior. Hites told the Bloomington *Herald-Times* that the Bloomington levels weren't high enough to cause concern. But he added that they shouldn't be ignored. "They're not lethal levels," he said. "But it's hard to judge the subtle health effects."

John Foster was fourteen years old and a freshman at Bloomington's University High School in 1957 when the Westinghouse Electric Company set up its new capacitor-manufacturing plant on the far west side of town. America was at the height of its economic prosperity, and the vision was that industrial growth, and the need to provide electricity to power it, would continue forever. Westinghouse and the good-paying jobs it would provide were eagerly welcomed as a keystone in the economic foundation the town was trying to establish.

Because of the toxic chemicals used at the plant, the Westinghouse presence in the community turned out to be more of a nightmare than a dream. The capacitors produced there contained more than just oily, poisonous insulating fluids. They contained copper. Scavengers used to snatch capacitors from the dumps and either break them open on the spot to retrieve the copper or salvage them at their homes. In either case, they drained the oils, intensifying PCB contamination at the dumps and spreading it beyond.

Awareness of a PCB problem in Bloomington began in November 1975 when Westinghouse informed the city of "minimal" discharges of PCBs from the plant into the city sewer system. The city then discovered PCB contamination at its Winston-Thomas Sewage Treatment Plant south of town. In January of the next year, the EPA discovered PCBs in leachate oozing from area dumps and in runoff from the Westinghouse plant, as well as at Winston-Thomas.

In May 1980, the city hired Chicago lawyer Joseph Karaganis to represent it in negotiations with Westinghouse over contamination of city sewer lines and the treatment plant. In April 1981, after negotiations broke down, the city sued Westinghouse in federal court for $149 million. In June, PCBs were discovered at the city-owned Lemon Lane Landfill in a poor section on the city's northwest side. In October, the city added Lemon Lane to the lawsuit and upped the amount being sought in court to $329 million. Monsanto also was named as a defendant.

A year later, on October 11, 1983, Bloomington mayor Tomi Allison called a news conference to tell the town that a resolution to the toxic problem was at hand. Flanked by Westinghouse officials, the mayor said that the corporation had agreed to clean up PCB contamination from six area dumps, the treatment plant, and several polluted streams. Westinghouse planned to excavate PCB-contaminated soils and materials and incinerate them. The company would build the incinerator, which would be fueled by burning municipal solid waste generated by city homes and businesses and generate electricity as a by-product. It seemed like a win-win situation for everyone.

"This is a very happy day for us," the mayor beamed.

The city, along with state and federal negotiators, then hammered out a 108-page cleanup agreement with Westinghouse, called a consent decree, outlining the details. It was formally released to the public on December 3, 1984. Federal officials estimated that Westinghouse would spend $100 million on the cleanup, the largest settlement ever negotiated under the then five-year-old Superfund law.

The consent decree called on Westinghouse to perform remedial cleanup measures at some of the sites and to have the incinerator built by 1989. It had fifteen years from the time the incinerator was constructed to complete the cleanup. Nonhazardous incinerator ash could be disposed of in sanitary landfills. Hazardous ash would have to be disposed of, at Westinghouse expense, in hazardous-waste landfills. When the cleanup was completed, the city could either buy the incinerator and continue using it or require Westinghouse to disassemble it.

The seeds of discontent with the mayor and her incinerator, however, were sown early in the story. Frustrated by the secret nature of the negotiations, more than one hundred people, led by local activist Mike Andrews, held a sixties-style demonstration in June 1984 outside a closed-door meeting between city officials and their attorneys. Another hundred or so attended the EPA-sponsored hearing when the agreement's details were announced in December. Andrews prophetically vowed two days later, "The people of Bloomington are not going to allow this incinerator to be built."

Before the agreement could be finalized in court, it had to be approved by the city council, the county commissioners, and the county council. Amid deafening shouts of "No incinerator!" from protesters who packed the city council chambers and rushed it as the vote came, the council approved the agreement by an 8-1 vote in March 1985. Under less dramatic conditions, the county commissioners approved it 2-1 and the county council 5-2 in April. The agreement was signed by U.S. District Judge S. Hugh Dillin in August, giving it the force of federal law.

The next month a group of incinerator opponents, including John Foster, formed the Monroe County Environmental Coalition (MCEC) and hired local attorney David McCrea to represent local PCB victims.

⊛ ⊛ ⊛ ⊛

The MCEC was a grassroots group whose members tended to come from the politically active segments of Bloomington culture, not from traditional environmental groups such as the Audubon Society or Sierra Club. In fact, incineration still was being touted at that time by such national groups as preferable to landfills for waste disposal.

The consent decree, in fact, split the Bloomington environmental community. The Sassafras Audubon Society, traditionally the community's leading environmental group, came out in support of the agreement and its incinerator. The group's president told the *Herald-Times* in 1987: "We supported the city signing the consent decree because we felt we had an existing health threat that had to be dealt with. Certainly they are dangerous things, and there are a lot of concerns that need to be watched every step of the way. But we think it is possible to build an incinerator that can, with a reasonable margin of safety, clean up the existing health threat." He said the tradeoff between the quantity of toxic materials destroyed and the amount created in the process was acceptable.

The Bloomington/Monroe County League of Women Voters took a slightly more reserved approach. Its president told the paper at the same time that the group supported the cleanup agreement but not necessarily the incinerator. "We made a statement in March of 1985 to the Bloomington City Council that we support the consent decree because it calls for the removal of PCB-contaminated materials from the community," she said. "We felt that this was a beginning that, with some clarification and monitoring, might hopefully be a solution to the problem. . . . We're still not certain that incineration is the best technology. We haven't seen another one that can address the complexity of the material that we're dealing with."

Other groups, including the Indiana Public Interest Research Group (InPIRG) and the MCEC, already had reached inviolate conclusions.

InPIRG PCB project director Mick Harrison, who would become one of the incinerator's most devoted and effective opponents, succinctly summed up his group's opposition: "We're suggesting there's a risk to incineration. We think it's an unacceptable risk. It's a risk that's going to hurt a lot of people."

The MCEC's Jon Canada agreed, arguing that incineration in the presence of oxygen would create furans and dioxins, which are more toxic than PCBs. "The city should be seriously looking at other technologies to bargain with," he told the paper. "We're not advocating any technology now. We want to entomb the PCBs in environmental vaults, thereby containing the current problem while not creating a future problem."

John Foster was a co-chair of the MCEC, but he decided early on that he was not interested in the spotlight. He had spoken to a reporter once with the understanding that he didn't want to be quoted, and some of what he said was printed anyway. That experience helped convince John that he should work behind the scenes, researching technical information and helping to develop strategy. "I did not want publicity, period," he says. "I have tried to stay behind others all along."

Almost from the outset, MCEC members decided that education was going to have to be their focus. The public had to be informed about the dangers of the proposed Bloomington incinerator. So did the politicians who supported it. Most of them, John says, hadn't even read the cleanup agreement and voted for it out of fear. High-priced lawyers had convinced them they could be held liable for the PCB contamination around the community. "Somewhere along the line it was just a matter of deciding, 'Okay, we're going to have to re-educate them because we can't overthrow them,'" John says.

Before opponents could re-educate local politicians, they had to educate themselves. They looked to others in the field of environmental activism for support and education. "I was running all over the country going to hazardous-waste conferences and meeting just about every known environmentalist in the United States that I could get any help from," John says. He was part of a Bloomington contingent that went to a conference in 1985 sponsored by the Citizens Clearinghouse for Hazardous Waste, the group formed by Love Canal's Lois Gibbs. "We started making contacts and learning how to deal with getting screwed by the politics of the whole thing."

On occasion, John infiltrated the enemy to further his education. From 1985 to 1989 he was a member of the Hazardous Materials Control Institute, which gained him access to conferences for industry he otherwise would have been kept out of. "I went to the meetings where the EPA and state officials and industry people were taught how to deal with people like me," he laughs.

After the company John worked for eliminated his department, leaving him without a job, he figured out a way to build on his base of knowledge and still fight the incinerator. He worked as a consultant for attorney David McCrea, researching toxic chemicals and helping McCrea prepare for lawsuits on behalf of former Westinghouse workers.

"I started reading every rag I could put my hands on that had to do with chemicals or PCBs," he says. "All of a sudden there was just more information about heavy metals and incinerators than anybody realized. Actually, I found out a whole lot of stuff early on from industry publications."

The more John read about chemicals and combustion, the more he realized that incineration was just one big experiment. If you don't know exactly what's going in the machine, you don't know what's coming out. And he was convinced that, for the most part, much of what's going to come out shouldn't.

John and the core group of activists through the years took several approaches to their educational efforts. They attended meetings and challenged elected and appointed officials with responsibility for the cleanup, they conducted massive letter-writing campaigns, they lobbied the public one on one.

Probably the most public activity John engaged in in all of the years he worked on the incinerator issue was attending public meetings. From the outset, John and the MCEC decided that someone had to be at every meeting to monitor what public officials were doing with regard to the cleanup agreement. And because of the technical nature of his research, John attended about every one so that he could present his information and challenge the positions put forth by those with positions contrary to his own. While he couldn't possibly estimate how many hours he spent at such meetings, John confidently puts it in the thousands. He attended every meeting of the city's Utilities Service Board for more than two years.

John also spent countless hours on the word processor, cranking out letters. He wrote to government officials apprising them of his findings. He wrote to other environmentalists, keeping them abreast of developments in Bloomington and carrying on a dialogue about how to fight their fights. He and others mounted a massive letter-to-the-editor campaign with the local paper. The goal was to have at least one letter in the paper each week. "Keeping it in the public eye, keeping things churned up, that was really what it was," he explains. "It was a constant letter-writing campaign. And we didn't just hit the local people; I communicated with people in the Justice Department, EPA, and IDEM. A whole lot of what I did behind the scenes was corresponding."

The letter-writing campaign wasn't aimed only at education. It had strategic aspects to it as well. One of the things John learned early from the CCHW's Lois Gibbs was that anytime a government agency receives a written request for information from a citizen or citizen group, it has to respond in writing. So, knowing that answering letters was a time-consuming endeavor, John and his cohorts kept a steady flow of requests in the mail to keep their opponents busy. "For quite some time IDEM and the EPA were just flooded with letters asking for bits and pieces of information," he says. "Somebody has to go and dig that information out and send it back to you in a letter-type form. So we were eating up a lot of their time to try and slow them down, to try and stall the process. We felt time was the only thing that we had that we could win with. We'd actually, out of our little core group, generate fourteen or fifteen letters a week and get those out to various government officials."

Letter writing wasn't the only way John tried to get the message out to the public and politicians. He also took his message to them face to face.

In March 1985, just before the Bloomington City Council was scheduled to vote on the consent decree, incinerator opponents initiated an anti-incinerator petition drive to show just how much the public was opposed to the plan. "I spent mega-hours standing outside the post office getting signatures on petitions and talking to people about the consent decree," he says. The result was that on March 21, just before the council voted, opponents produced petitions containing 7,769 signatures, more signatures than there had been votes cast for Mayor Allison or any council member in the 1983 election.

On August 22, 1986, the MCEC and InPIRG released several hundred black balloons from the proposed incinerator site to show how far pollution would be carried. The balloons had notes on them asking whoever found them to contact the MCEC or InPIRG. "We got several responses back from Ohio and a couple from Kentucky," John says.

John and the MCEC in 1986 began having incinerator opponents occupy booths at the county fair, a tradition that continued throughout the entire battle. John, who helped out in the booth for all but a couple of years, says that they would try and get a spot somewhere in between the Democrat and Republican booths so that they could get their points across to anyone who displayed an interest in politics. "There were people who didn't even know there were toxic problems or a proposed incinerator here in the county," he says.

In 1987, John began leading what he called the "Toxic Tour." He would take anyone who was interested on a guided tour of Bloomington's contaminated sites. The tour would begin on Bloomington's poor west side, where most of the contamination spread by scavenging was located, visit the various landfills and dumps where PCBs had been dumped, pass by the incinerator site, stop at the polluted Winston-Thomas Sewage Treatment Plant, and eventually end up at the farm of Dale and Connie Conard. The Conards lived next to a contaminated landfill and had had hundreds of deformed pigs born on their farm through the years. There were pigs with deformed limbs, without skin, missing eyes or pupils, without anuses. Several were stored in their freezer, and John would unwrap the pigs from the plastic they were encased in and hand them to whoever was taking the tour. "I can't prove that PCBs had anything to do with those pigs being deformed," he says. "But something coming out of that landfill did. It might have been crass to just hand them to people, but it did have an effect."

Between 1985 and 1991, John conducted dozens of Toxic Tours for politicians, including Senator Dan Coats; candidates for elective office; environmentalists, including a busload of Greenpeace activists; and the general public. "It's probably something I did about thirty or forty times," he says. Eventually, John got a letter from the EPA telling him to stop because Westinghouse had reported that he had been seen inside the fences at Superfund sites, a charge that he vehemently denies. He also got a call from the sheriff, saying that he would be prosecuted if he didn't stop. "I've never done that in my life. I would never take anyone into a Superfund fenced area," he says. "Now, if it's stuff outside the fence that should be fenced, then I have taken them on site. I got so hot over that until I realized there was nothing I could do but just let it go. There was no point in it." Not wanting to push things beyond that level, John formally stopped conducting Toxic Tours.

The proposed incinerator had two significant weaknesses that John and opponents capitalized on. It was being considered at a time when incineration as a technology was coming under increasing fire as a cure as bad as or worse than the disease. And it was, as the U.S. Office of Technology Assessment said in September 1986, a "novel but unproven" technology. There simply weren't any incinerators of its kind anywhere in the world.

Incineration had gained popularity in the early 1970s as an alternative to nasty, leaky landfills. Environmental groups had made landfills Public Enemy Number One in the waste-disposal arena. And as landfills, particularly in the urban Northeast, began to fill up and siting new ones became difficult because of public opposition, incinerators became the preferred alternative. The attractiveness of modern, energy-producing resource-recovery incinerators was further enhanced by the Arab oil embargo of the 1970s. Not only were they seen as a way to safely dispose of garbage, but they also could help reduce America's dependence on foreign energy.

By 1987, industry sources estimated that there were sixty-seven trash incinerators in operation in the United States, thirty under construction, thirty-five in advanced planning stages, and two hundred more proposed.

However, incineration had begun to lose its appeal for some environmentalists in the late 1970s when European researchers discovered dioxins in waste-incinerator emissions. Karen Shapiro, a researcher with Barry Commoner's Center for the Biology of Natural Systems at Queens College in New York, put the problem in perspective. "We now know that all municipal waste incinerators emit dioxin and that the dioxin is formed in the incinerator," she told the *Herald-Times* in 1987. "It's sort of like a dioxin-producing factory."

Incinerator proponents argued that pollution-control equipment, if properly installed and operated, could capture dioxins and other pollutants and keep them from being released into the air. But Shapiro and incinerator opponents countered that that would only shift the burden back to landfills. "Actually, incinerators are not getting rid of the need for a landfill but are perpetuating it and, in fact, might require a need for more hazardous-waste landfills," Shapiro said.

Questions about the novel approach of burning trash and hazardous waste in the same incinerator gained John and incinerator opponents an important political ally fairly early in the fight. While Mayor Allison was digging in her heels, defending the consent decree as the only way locals could have any chance of preventing an unsafe incinerator from being built, county commissioners president Charlotte Zietlow was wavering. At first she supported the idea, telling the paper it seemed "maybe it was a step in the right direction."

John says it had become clear almost from day one that not only had most of the local officials not read anything about PCBs or incineration, but only a handful had even read the consent decree. They were listening to the lawyers and experts hired by the city who said that the agreement was in the community's best interests, that the consent decree gave the community an opportunity to have significant input into whether the incinerator would be acceptable or not. Zietlow, he says, was among those who had read the consent decree and, more important, was willing to consider the information John and others were generating.

John says he spent countless hours and dollars duplicating information and articles and feeding them to Zietlow. "She was the first elected person who actually sat down and read critical information and was able to understand it, or was intelligent enough to understand it," he says. "And she was willing to work at it. Scientifically she could understand what she was reading, and that this incinerator was bad, and that we really didn't want to do this. And, as she had said, it took her a while, but once she had that feeling in her gut, she went with it."

Zietlow became one of only four elected officials to vote against the consent decree. She explained her reservations to the newspaper: "I wanted to be a good girl and go along with the crowd. But on the other hand, I just thought there was something wrong. I didn't like it."

Three months after her vote against the consent decree, Zietlow organized a trip for local officials and media representatives to visit hazardous-waste incinerators in Deer Park, Texas, and El Dorado, Arkansas. She was struck during that trip by how careful the operators were about what went into their machines. When she contrasted that with the plans for Bloomington—digging up entire decades-old landfills and putting dirt and trash and PCBs into an incinerator fueled by burning trash—she got scared. Such a technology had never been tried anywhere in the world.

"I think I understand the technology reasonably well, better than most people in this community, to be sure," she told the *Herald-Times.* "I'm not a scientist, and I'm not an engineer, and I may be wrong. But I'm not stupid, and I've done a lot of research, and I'm skeptical of the technology, very much."

Zietlow's emerging opposition to the incinerator legitimized the anti-incinerator position, which prior to that time had largely been seen as coming from radical political activists. In 1987, she vested the opposition with weight that would carry it almost to the mayor's office. She challenged fellow Democrat Allison in the mayoral primary, making the incinerator the centerpiece of her campaign. She came within seventy-five votes of unseating the popular mayor, who went on to re-election in 1987 and again in 1991.

While several anti-incinerator candidates ran for office in 1987, only two were elected—Democrats Patrick Murphy, who had voted against the consent decree in 1985, and newcomer Lin Gardner. But Zietlow's effort set a new tone for Monroe County politics. From that point forward, the politically correct position for a candidate to take was anti-incinerator. Three years later, in March 1990, Allison herself wrote to Westinghouse, saying that the incinerator posed unacceptable health risks and should be scrapped.

John gives credit to both Zietlow and Gardner for the changing attitudes toward the incinerator among politicians and the public. Using her position on the council, Gardner kept the incinerator issue in the public eye. And she had contacts within the EPA who leaked information to her. "We actually knew what was happening down here before they did in Chicago," John says. "I had access to all kinds of information."

Zietlow's effort in the primary probably turned the tide of public opinion against the incinerator. Her running on an anti-incinerator platform and nearly upsetting a powerful mayor in her own party's primary added credibility to the movement and brought new people to it. "You've got to look that at least half the people in her own party thought Tomi was wrong," John says. "Charlotte gets a lot of credit for that. It was a ballsy move."

Unquestionably, the death knell for the incinerator began sounding in April 1989, when Westinghouse announced that it would construct a hazardous-waste landfill in Monroe County for the incinerator's ash. Ten months later, amid rumors that the company was looking at property near the Indiana 37 Bypass north of Bloomington, a handful of residents in the landfill area held a meeting to discuss what they could do to keep their neighborhood toxics-free. John was away at an environmental conference in Denver when that first meeting was held. Several people had told those who put the meeting together that they needed to contact him. So when John got back, they called another meeting. "They were basically like a little business group," he says. "They wanted to know what they had to do to stop the landfill. And I said, 'Well, the first thing you have to do is stop the incinerator, because if you don't stop the incinerator, there's definitely going to be a landfill.'"

The small group of people who had met at Mike Baker's rural Monroe County home that Sunday evening formed the core of the newest anti-incinerator group in Bloomington, the Coalition Opposed to PCB Ash in Monroe County, or COPA. The group wanted to know how many votes it would need to swing the 1991 city elections. John said fifteen hundred. But instead of focusing on electoral politics, he told them that they needed to focus on public education.

One of the group's members, Jim Shea, met with the mayor a couple of times, getting the same reception that John had five years earlier. "Basically, he told her, 'Well then, we are going to turn Bloomington pink and black,'" John says, referring to the COPA colors. "That's when we started handing out bumper stickers and yard signs and putting up billboards."

Prior to that time, the debate over incineration had been primarily scientific, with experts on both sides of the argument providing conflicting evidence that overwhelmed the average person. While the passion and logic of a handful of activists like John had successfully swayed significant public and political opinion against the incinerator, the process had simply been put on hold. But the threat posed by a hazardous-waste landfill was tangible. It threatened not just public health, but property values as well.

Under the leadership of veterans such as John and newcomers such as Baker, COPA broadened the spectrum of anti-incinerator activists to include property owners, business people, farmers, country folk, and conservatives. "COPA was great because it was another whole group of people," John says. "People started listening because all of a sudden it was people in suits and ties that were talking instead of ex-hippies or whatever."

Consistent with his role throughout, John remained behind the scenes. COPA people picked up where others had left off in the letter-writing campaign. John did research and fed it to those writing letters and taking the fight to the public and the politicians.

A major difference between COPA and the MCEC, People Against the Incinerator, InPIRG, and other anti-incinerator groups that had sprung up through the years in Bloomington was that COPA people had money. And they spared no expense in their efforts at painting Bloomington pink and black.

"No Incinerator" yard signs and bumper stickers began appearing throughout the county. On the day of the first IU football game that fall of 1990, yard signs were placed every two hundred feet down the median of Indiana 37 between Bloomington and Martinsville. COPA printed up a professional twelve-page pink and black booklet called "Bloomington at Risk: No Incinerator, Stop

Toxic Dump," which outlined the evils of the incinerator. About twenty thousand were distributed throughout the community and state, and copies were mailed to every member of the Hoosier Environmental Council. John penned perhaps the booklet's most effective and remembered section. The heading on one page read, "Communities That Have Had Positive Experiences with Incinerators." The page was blank. The opposite page's heading said, "Communities That Have Had Problems with Incinerators." The text ran into the margins and off the bottom of the page.

COPA members kept up the tradition of having a booth at the county fair and went to talk to neighborhood associations, schools, sewing circles, and any other group that would have them, to spread their message. As John told the *Herald-Times* in March 1994, "You can accomplish a lot with billboards, yard signs, and thousands of fliers."

Suddenly, Democrats and Republicans were trying to outdo each other in opposing the incinerator. Allison's letter to Westinghouse came within two months of COPA's formation. State senator Vi Simpson and state representative Mark Kruzan, both Democrats and long-time incinerator foes, sponsored legislation in the 1991 legislative session that prohibited the state from issuing permits for the incinerator until it had conducted a two-year study of alternative technologies. The bill was signed into law by Governor Evan Bayh in May.

In June, congressman Frank McCloskey wrote to the EPA opposing the incinerator and urging the agency to study alternative technologies. Also in June, the city council, county commissioners, and county council all passed resolutions opposing the incinerator. This time all but one of the nineteen elected officials on the three boards voted against the incinerator. And the one who voted no said that he opposed the incinerator but couldn't support the resolution.

Between July and October 1991, Westinghouse applied for the necessary state permits for the incinerator and landfill, knowing that they wouldn't be touched for two years. A year later, in November 1992, Westinghouse announced that the earliest the incinerator could be up and running would be 1998, nine years after the timetable set forth by the consent decree.

By 1993, it was clear that even Westinghouse had given up on the incinerator. The company's silence was conspicuous as Simpson- and Kruzan-sponsored legislation that effectively guaranteed that the incinerator would not be built breezed through the legislature. The bill called on the company to prove in advance that its incinerator could destroy 99.9999 percent of all the PCBs that went through it, a daunting if not impossible requirement. The bill passed and was signed into law by Governor Bayh.

❧ ❧ ❧ ❧

Nearly a decade after Mayor Allison's press conference announcing plans for the incinerator, the high-tech machine that had torn the community apart without ever having been built was for all practical purposes pronounced dead. Representatives from the city, the county, the state, the EPA, and Westinghouse held a news conference in Bloomington on February 11, 1994, to announce that they were essentially starting over. The consent decree allows Westinghouse to propose alternatives to Judge Dillin. And city spokesman John Langley said the judge had been informed that the parties were jointly going to study alternatives to the incinerator.

The consent decree remains in place. But officials said that they would evaluate each of the consent decree sites and all of the existing information on the situation, and if acceptable forms of treatment are found, they would work through the court to make the necessary changes to the agreement. They stressed that the announcement did not mean the incinerator was dead. But that was clear to everyone in the community.

Standing in the background, wearing a coat and tie and smiling smugly, was John Foster. John says that several things were going through his mind while the news conference was underway. He wondered whether the officials thought that the public might forget that the same legal agreement that almost brought the incinerator to Bloomington would still control the process. He wondered what the public would think about the $5 million that Langley said the city had spent on the consent decree, only to have the process return to the beginning. And he thought about Westinghouse and whether the public would trust the company in the new round of discussions. "As far as I'm concerned," he says, "Westinghouse has lied to us from day one. I don't trust them."

John says he does believe that the garbage-fired incinerator is dead. The case against the combination of technologies is overwhelming. And Westinghouse has indicated that it couldn't afford to fuel the incinerator with natural gas. The consent decree called for Westinghouse to be paid a per-ton fee for burning the garbage equal to what the city would have paid to have it landfilled. "Now, of course, the judge could say you will fire it with natural gas and I don't care what it costs, but I don't think the chances of that happening are too heavy," John says.

But John doesn't necessarily believe that the community is out of the woods as far as incineration goes. "I don't know where we stand right now," he says. "I'm not quite as convinced as everybody else that there won't still be some kind of an incinerator or an incineration process. It might be an on-site incinerator, but there could be one."

The son of an Indiana University education professor, John was born and raised in Bloomington. He attended IU, studying fine arts with an eye toward becoming either a sculptor or a sculpture teacher. Toward the end of his undergraduate training, he began working part-time for Hoosier Energy as a civil engineer. When he was offered a full-time job, John calculated that he was being offered more than his father was making after teaching for twenty years. "That changed my mind about teaching real quick, just real quick," he says. "It was strictly money." He later was hired by the Ralph Rogers Group in Bloomington, where he worked as an engineer and mechanic for the next seventeen years. That's where he was employed when he was first exposed to PCBs at Bennett's Quarry.

John may have taken the path that led to money, but he still looks the part of an artist. He's of average height, lean, with sculpted features and a neatly trimmed salt-and-pepper beard that he constantly strokes while relating the story of his decade fighting the Bloomington incinerator. It's easy to visualize him striking the same pose while developing an approach to a mound of clay or a chunk of bronze. He speaks thoughtfully, methodically, punctuating his story with a baritone laugh from time to time when his discourse exposes the sheer stupidity of the Bloomington incinerator. He lives with Deidre, his wife of ten years, in a two-story frame house on a wooded lot a few miles north of Bloomington, and just north of the proposed Westinghouse landfill site.

John is blessed with mechanical skills that he deftly uses to restore antique cars. While working with the Rogers Group, he restored the company president's antique car collection. In his own basement is a 1961 XKE Jaguar that he bought new, hasn't driven since 1978, and plans to restore. "Yeah, I'm a funny guy," he says. "I've recycled and reused stuff all my life. If I can give something a second or third life, I do it. There's no need to throw it away."

The redbuds and dogwoods were in bloom and the sun was turning the western sky reddish-yellow as we sat on his screened-in porch, serenaded by chirping insects and birds, and talked about the incinerator fiasco.

John sees the efforts at educating the public and the politicians as key to finally prevailing in the ten-year incinerator war. The early acts of guerrilla theater by incinerator opponents were useful in capturing public attention and mobilizing early opposition. And they were effective in their own way. "If it hadn't been for those guys at the beginning, we would have an incinerator burning down there right now," he says. "They brought the attention out the best way they knew how."

But that just isn't John's way of doing things. He's a researcher and a talker. He is willing to spend as long as it takes to educate first himself and then others. "You can get things accomplished by talking," he says. "I'm a great believer that the only way you can change someone's mind is through education. Believe me, there have been people in this town who have done a total about-face after just listening to me. It might take a couple of hours. But eventually, they can see what happened and is happening in Bloomington."

But that's not to say that John always maintained his cool as he hit the wall over and over again with politicians bound and determined to thwart him. "There was a time when I was angry, and I shouted a lot, and I'd lose it at meetings," he says. "And whenever I'd do that, I'd get mad at myself because I'd think, 'They can see that I'm irritated. They know they're getting to me.'"

The dedication and never-give-up attitude of the core group of incinerator opponents made the difference, he believes. They were at meetings, providing documents to public officials, making sure they were as educated on the issues as the opponents were. "It just became obvious to me real early on that when citizens aren't around, all kinds of funny things happen," he says. "Somewhere along the line I realized that you really just couldn't trust them."

🏵 🏵 🏵 🏵

Attorney McCrea has known John since junior high school. And he says that there was probably no one single individual more qualified than John to tackle a complicated issue such as the Bloomington incinerator. He brought to the struggle a unique combination of character traits—intellect, patience, and compassion—that guaranteed he would be a positive force in the effort.

Of critical importance was John's ability to understand the complicated social and political issues of the incinerator fight along with the dense technical and engineering aspects. "John combined this intellectual capacity with a very practical, hands-on type application," McCrea says. "Here's a guy who has the intellect to absorb complex issues, but in junior high school he was putting a 1954 Chrysler Firepower engine in a 1938 Ford, with the accelerator controlled by a chain. I mean, you don't have too many people like that. He could sit there and look at four hundred wires all going from someplace to someplace, which would totally confound and confuse 99.999 percent of the people, and he had the patience to sit there and figure out each and every wire."

John's patience contributed heavily to his ability to sway people to his point of view on the incinerator, McCrea says. He's careful and analytical in his preparation. He doesn't leave himself open to challenge because he is thoroughly prepared and convinced of his position before he makes public statements. "He's a person with a tremendous amount of pride," McCrea says. "Everything he did, whether it was building hot rods in high school or managing a multi-million-dollar inventory of heavy equipment for Ralph Rogers or whatever work he was involved in, he was a perfectionist."

McCrea attributes John's incredible stamina in the incinerator battle to his early experience and his unselfish attitude toward life. Not only was John convinced that the Neal's Landfill remediation was inadequate, he also knew that it had direct victims, the Conards. "The combination of knowing firsthand what was taking place and then seeing the predicament and suffering of really good people provided his inspiration," McCrea says.

"John is definitely, positively, and unequivocally unique in his capacity, interest, skills, and intellect," McCrea says. "He just doesn't make mistakes. If they had listened to John Foster, they would have been miles ahead, dollars ahead, and this community would be in a much stronger position than it is now. There's no reason why a person like John Foster should not have been listened to."

❦ ❦ ❦ ❦

By the time we sat down to talk in the spring of 1994, John Foster said that he had reached the point of burnout. There had been several years where everything he did was PCB-related. A rule in the Foster home was that there had to be an agreement before PCBs could be discussed. "It got to the point where it was almost like a cancer," John says. "It just ate up my entire life."

Still, he remains active because of his commitment to the cause and his working relationship with COPA's Mike Baker. Baker now does the bulk of the work, so John doesn't have to. And his style provides a good counterpoint to John's. They often play good-cop-bad-cop in their approach to the city or Westinghouse or EPA. "He's always kind of like a salesman and happy-go-lucky," John says. "I get a little sterner with my voice than he does. Mike has developed a relationship with these people. They're friends. I'm polite to almost all of those people, but they're not my friends. We're adversaries."

John has several pieces of advice for those who find themselves faced with environmental nightmares such as the proposed Bloomington incinerator. Foremost among them is to find out everything there is to know about the opposition. And in contrast to the situation in 1982 when he first became concerned about toxic contamination in Bloomington, today there are numerous resources that neophyte environmental activists can turn to. "Talk to other environmental groups, that's real important," he says. "I can't think of anything right now, be it a particular chemical or some waste company or somebody working on a landfill, that somebody, somewhere, doesn't have a history about them already."

Networking with groups such as PAHLS and Citizens Clearinghouse for Hazardous Waste can have a number of advantages, not the least of which is getting assistance to build a case. "At this point in time, industry trains people, and so does EPA, in how to handle meetings, crowd situations," he says. "I have a network of friends all through the United States, and we all share newsletters and can help each other out on different things. You have to make sure you can back everything up scientifically with paper. There's a group out east that I'm on their professional board for PCBs, because if there's anything they need, I can tell them where to get it." Other groups can provide other types of support as well. CCHW has meetings at which people who have burned out can help each other.

"The main thing is to get involved and don't be afraid of politicians," John says. "Just remember that it may be city hall, but they get up and get dressed every morning the same way that you do. Don't be afraid to meet them one to one all the way up to the president if need be. I've gone to Washington, I think, eight times. The first couple of times I did it I was kind of overwhelmed with Washington and its greatness inside the loop. But as time went on I realized, 'Hey, I am actually paying these people's salaries. They have to listen to me.' So, I wouldn't worry about telling anyone to question authority. It's really that simple."

⹁

JOHN   BLAIR

No matter what John Blair decides to do in defense of the Indiana environment, he does it with flair. Whether he is giving the press what it needs for a lead story, challenging his colleagues in the environmental movement to be bold, or getting arrested to make a point, John Blair is dramatic. As a founder of and the energy behind the Evansville-based Valley Watch, John has led the charge against several environmental abominations proposed for his beloved Ohio River Valley, including plans in the mid-1970s to make the area a center for the synthetic fuels industry. His greatest achievements as an environmentalist include his work against the Marble Hill Nuclear Power Plant. A journalism teacher and Pulitzer Prize–winning photographer, John used his journalistic skills as a weapon against the plant and its supporters. He carried the anti–Marble Hill, anti–nuclear power message to thousands by publishing a newspaper called *OVE* (Ohio Valley Environment). His reporting on the issue is credited by many as a key tool in the successful fight against the plant. John, forty-eight, lives in Evansville with his wife, Mary, and two children, Stephanie and Will. He runs a photo studio and works as a freelance photographer for newspapers and news magazines.

JOHN BLAIR

Watching the Valley

⊰⊰ ⊰⊰ ⊰⊰ ⊰⊰ 8 John Blair first came to the Ohio River Valley in 1974 to teach. And that is what he
has spent the past twenty years doing,
though not in the way that originally
brought him to Evansville. After earning a master's degree at Ball
State, John was hired by the University of Evansville to teach
journalism. But his unwillingness to keep his opinions to himself
ensured that that job wouldn't last long. His politics did him in.

It was during the city's preparation for the Bicentennial celebration that John Blair first opened his mouth in public in Evansville. Movers and shakers in the state's third-largest city were
planning a tribute to the nation's two-hundredth anniversary.
They were going to construct what they called the "Four Free-
doms Monument" in downtown Evansville. It would have had
four pillars with aluminum pennants in honor of Alcoa Aluminum, a major Evansville-area industry, with an eternal flame
burning. Not only did John think that the entire project looked
stupid, he was appalled at the lack of environmental awareness.
"This was in the middle of the energy crisis, in 1975, and they
were going to have an eternal flame just wasting this natural gas,"
he says.

At a public meeting, John called for a public debate on what
the project should be, saying that freedom is about free speech,
not being dictated to by the powers that be. John says he now

realizes who was present the night he stood up to challenge the project—"the city fathers; I mean, every one of them was in the room." The power structure had never been challenged in that way before, he says. The result was that the monument wasn't built as planned. And he was not rehired to teach a third year at the university. In his mind, losing his job was the direct result of his speaking out.

Shortly after that, John began his second career as a teacher. Surrounded by the beauty of the Ohio River on his boat one summer day, John had an epiphany that his role in life was to educate the public about the environment and the Ohio River Valley. That was the moment that John says he became a true environmentalist. His first step along his new path was to run for Congress in the Democratic primary in 1976, making the environment in general and the proposed Wabash River Barge Canal in particular his issues. John lost that race but stayed active in the canal issue, which environmentalists finally defeated in early 1977.

Shortly thereafter, John learned that the federal Energy Research and Development Administration was considering a section of the Hoosier National Forest as a possible site for storing nuclear waste. In response, he formed a group called the Nuclear Waste Action Committee, which was a small but committed group of "ragtag hippies" dedicated to stopping the waste plan. Among the people who got involved in the issue were two who would become John's closest friends and collaborators in the eco-battles to come—Tom Zeller and Doug Keil. They rallied support in Tell City and in short order had the mayor, the chamber of commerce, even the banks on their side. The NWAC decided to have a protest rally near Tell City in July 1977; they put up posters in the area and publicized the event around the state. The day before the rally was to be held, Indiana senator Birch Bayh's office announced that the energy administration had abandoned plans for the Hoosier. The NWAC went ahead with the rally, and John Blair was hooked on environmental activism. For the first time in his life, speaking out had spelled victory for him, not disaster. "Here's the Wabash Canal and then the nuclear waste site," he says. "Two victories, and we hadn't put that much effort into it. It had been an effort. But it hadn't been anything to wear any of us out. That was enough to launch us."

Blair, Zeller, and Keil began looking for another issue, which didn't take long to find. In September 1977, two months after the nuclear sites were abandoned by the government, the Nuclear

Regulatory Commission held public hearings on Public Service
Indiana's proposed Marble Hill Nuclear Generating Station.
"I got involved in Marble Hill," John says.

The struggle over Marble Hill was four years old when John
Blair entered the fray. PSI, the state's largest utility, had announced plans to go nuclear in 1973 with a 2.26 million kilowatt
nuclear plant to be constructed on a bluff overlooking John's
beloved Ohio River about ten miles southwest of Madison. The
plant was to be located on the 987-acre site of a nineteenth-century marble mine. PSI's stated goal was to ensure a steady supply
of energy for PSI customers in sixty-nine counties.

PSI owned an 83 percent interest in the Marble Hill plant. The
Wabash Valley Power Association, which represented twenty-one
rural electric cooperatives, owned the other 17 percent. The price
tag, according to PSI in 1973, was $792 million. The massive con-
tainment buildings that would have housed the plant's two
nuclear reactors were to be 200 feet high and 140 feet wide, with
4-foot-thick concrete walls. In September 1975, PSI applied to the
Nuclear Regulatory Commission for a permit to begin construction on Marble Hill. The first reactor was scheduled to go on line
in 1982, the second in 1984.

As was the case elsewhere across the country, opposition to
nuclear power in Indiana grew along with progress toward an
operating plant. Among the opposition were two highly public
citizen groups—the Paddlewheel Alliance, a loosely organized six-
ties-type group, and Save the Valley, a tight-knit, sophisticated
group headed by intellectuals centered in the Madison area.

The Paddlewheel Alliance focused its efforts on civil disobedience, carrying out two occupations of the plant site in 1978 and
1979 that resulted in the arrests of 130 protesters. Save the Valley,
under the influence of people such as Fred Hauck, an engineer
from Shelbyville, Kentucky; Bob Gray, an insurance adjuster from
Hanover; and Harold Cassidy, a professor emeritus at Hanover
College, attacked the plant from an intellectual perspective. Hauck
in particular focused his efforts on the economics of the plant and
the utility, constantly challenging PSI's financial projections. By
1978, before construction had even begun, PSI had spent $2 mil-
lion on Marble Hill. At that time, the utility was estimating the
project cost at $1.86 billion, more than twice its original estimate.

John involved himself in both groups, finding his six-month involvement with Paddlewheel to be "the most god-awful experience I've ever had." The organization, which was formed right after a September 1977 public hearing on the startup of construction, was democratic to the point of being dysfunctional, John says. Everyone was an equal in Paddlewheel, and anyone could break the group's consensus, which was required to make a decision. "I sat through these meetings that would last for ten and twelve hours at a time, and nothing would be decided," he says. "I just said to hell with this. I'm not participating in this."

To John's way of thinking, activist groups need to be small, with like-minded people who can make decisions and follow through on them. That is how he says Save the Valley worked. And that's where he learned to be an effective activist. "I have complete love, devotion, and respect for Save the Valley," he says. "They will always remain in my heart as the people who showed me the way. So anything I have to say about Marble Hill has to be prefaced with that."

John's work as a photographer and his love of the Ohio River contributed greatly to his decision to devote his life to the Marble Hill debate and environmental activism. After losing his job at the University of Evansville, he became a freelance photographer. A major portion of his meager income came from stringing for the United Press International, the *Evansville Press, Newsweek*, and other publications.

For some time John had been developing an interest in energy issues, in particular the proliferation of power plants in the tri-state area. "It just seemed like every week you turned around and a new power plant was being proposed in this place or that place in Indiana, Illinois, or Kentucky," he says. That interest continued to grow with three assignments he had in 1977 and 1978—photographing a strip mine in Dugger; shooting pictures for stories on the Strip Mine Act of 1977, which were used in congressional hearings on abandoned mines; and covering the 1978 coal strike for *Newsweek*.

But while John's interest in energy contributed to his commitment to stop Marble Hill, it was his love of the river that hooked him. "It was through a long process of other venues and ventures that I ended up here in Evansville," he says while sitting on the riverside just downstream from a city water-intake pipe. "But I fell in love with the river, and that is what has kept me here. And Marble Hill was on the river. I started reading about things like strontium 90 and tritium that are routinely released from nuclear power plants in water. I knew that water was going to make its way here. I was able to visualize this strontium and tritium and whatever else floating down the river and being taken in by that water pipe. I didn't think it was very wise to put our water supply at risk from a thing like Marble Hill."

John wasn't alone in that regard. The plant, which would have been located thirty miles upstream from Louisville, had a pipe that would have discharged sixty-three gallons of water contaminated with minute amounts of at least thirty radioactive contaminants into the Ohio every second. The city of Louisville and the state of Kentucky were on record as opposing Marble Hill, in part because of the threat that it posed to Louisville's water supply.

John Blair had a solid foundation of knowledge, concern, and motivation to fight Marble Hill when the public hearing rolled around in September 1977, and he took the plunge, becoming active in both Save the Valley and the Paddlewheel Alliance. But it wasn't until a series of events a few months later that his role was defined.

First was a conservation he had with Save the Valley's Harold Cassidy. As much as John admired the group's leaders, they were saddled with a considerable handicap, he says. They were stalwart performers in their own ways, but they weren't very creative. "They worked their butts off," John says, "but they didn't know how to get the media, they didn't know how to raise the issue and make it a political issue, and I did."

But John was reluctant to move into a leadership role, and he expressed that sentiment to Cassidy during what turned out to be a life-changing conversation. "I can't remember where it was, or what I said, but he said, 'John, you're the one that's got to do it because you're the one with the energy.' And that really meant something to me because he recognized me as an equal, on his terms. Here he was, a Ph.D. and all this stuff. And I said, 'Well, Harold, maybe you're right.' I was talking about doing something real creative. I don't remember what it was, but he said, 'You're the one that's got to do it. You're the one that's got to lead the way.'"

About the same time, in early 1978, John Blair had a spiritual experience that he says also helped clear the way for his moving from the shadows to a position of leadership in the Marble Hill fight. "I'm not a real religious person," he says, "but all my life I've had these things happen to me, kind of religious experiences. And one of them was along about the same time that Harold basically handed me the reins. I was lying in bed one night, and it said, 'Trust your judgment, trust your own judgment.' It was a real clear voice, and it said repeatedly, 'Trust your own judgment.' It was like it was trying to put across a point to me, that I was on the right path."

Fast on the heels of that experience, John's photographic endeavors once again contributed to his environmental activities. In April 1978, John Blair won the Pulitzer Prize for photography for a photograph he had taken of Tony Kiritsis, the man who had lashed a shotgun to the neck of a loan officer in Indianapolis and held him captive. Bolstered by Cassidy's confidence, his own inner voice, and the notoriety that he received from the Pulitzer, John's career as an environmentalist took off. "I just unleashed a flurry of activity," he says, "and the rest is history."

❧ ❧ ❧ ❧

The flurry began with the creation of a publication called *OVE*, which stood for "Ohio Valley Environment." John served as publisher, editor, reporter, and photographer, as well as ad salesman. Zeller served as national editor, writing about issues such as acid rain and the Clean Air Act. Keil and others served in a variety of capacities.

The newspaper was started on the money that John received from his Pulitzer Prize and a thousand dollars donated by a man named Leon Pounds from Rockport, who had a group called Citizens to Save Spencer County that was fighting a proposed power plant in nearby Rockport. John had two goals for *OVE*—to defeat both Marble Hill and plans to develop a synthetic fuels industry in the Ohio Valley. "Three of them within twenty miles of where we sit," he says of the synfuels plants, "and they were horrors environmentally."

The *OVE*, published in an eleven-by-fifteen-inch format on newsprint, was lavishly illustrated with John's black-and-white photography. From February 1979 through 1982, 17,000 were published monthly, with the slogan "Free for Now" in the upper-right-hand corner. The approach they took was objective reporting, serious journalism. "We pledge to report fairly and accurately, but the scope of our coverage will favor the environment," John wrote by way of introduction in the first *OVE*. "It is our desire to serve as a communicative and educational tool for valley residents in pursuit of a livable environment. Success for the *OVE* will be measured, not by our assets, but by the quality of life in the OHIO VALLEY ENVIRONMENT."

John's focus on legitimate journalism brought criticism from some in the environmental movement, he says. But he believes that approach made the *OVE* a significant factor in the defeat of Marble Hill. Even though opponents knew that John would print outlandish things that they might say, they talked to him. And the *OVE* had a substantial number of important people on its mailing list—congressmen, senators, people such as Frank O'Bannon, then publisher of the Corydon *Democrat*. "When nobody else would report it, I would," John says. "At least we were getting the information out to the powers that be."

His efforts with *OVE* did not go unnoticed. In February 1981, Blair and *OVE* received the Knob and Valley Audubon Society's first annual award for "Outstanding Investigative Reporting" for a story about federal subsidies on Marble Hill. "He was the first person to uncover the fact that one federal agency continued to pump large sums of money into the project while another federal agency had forced most construction to stop because of construction defects," an Audubon spokesman was quoted as saying.

During a visit to Evansville in June 1980, Ralph Nader was asked by someone in the audience how people could get involved. "And Ralph said, 'Well let me show you how a couple of people got involved,'" John says. "And he holds up a copy of the *OVE* and he said, 'This is the finest publication I've ever seen of its type. In fact, I don't think I've ever seen anything of its type.'"

John was also instrumental in the formation of a variety of groups to take on different issues and functions. Among them was Valley Watch, formed in February 1981, which would serve as John's home base for more than a decade, long after *OVE* had ceased publishing. "It was almost like a big multinational corporation operating at the local level," John says. "We would form all these organizations. We had one called the Southern Indiana Environmental Political Action Coalition to endorse candidates and things like that. A lot of it was the same people. But we formed these different little entities to perform different tasks. And we were all over the place. It was amazing how much energy we had."

To fight the synfuel plants, John, Zeller, and a group of educators, lawyers, and health-care professionals formed a group called Synfuel Inquiry. "Frankly, Synfuel Inquiry defined synfuels nationally," John says.

꙳ ꙳ ꙳ ꙳

Construction on the Marble Hill plant, and the public debate over it, were well underway by the time the first *OVE* was published in February 1979. The Nuclear Regulatory Commission had given plant construction the go-ahead in April 1978, to the delight of PSI and politicians supporting nuclear power in Indiana.

Republican Hoosier senator Richard Lugar, for example, praised the NRC decision, seizing upon the ongoing coal strike at the time as proof that Indiana needed nukes to decrease its dependence on coal for energy. Even the near-disaster at Three Mile Island in March 1979 failed to budge powerful Hoosier politicians from their support for nuclear power. Republican governor Otis Bowen in an April 1979 speech cast the TMI "incident" in the context of "acceptable risk, which we apply every time we get into our family automobile or step into a bathtub," John reported in the *OVE*.

Opponents of the project had likewise become unyielding in their positions. In October 1978, thirty-one Paddlewheel Alliance protesters were arrested as they climbed over fences at the Marble Hill construction site in one of the largest acts of mass civil disobedience the state had seen since the Vietnam War days. Their trial showed that the general public, at least in the Madison area, was just as divided. Twenty-nine protesters went to trial on trespassing charges in January 1979. A five-man, one-woman jury deliberated five hours before telling the judge that they couldn't reach a verdict. The judge declared a mistrial. The Jefferson County prosecutor decided not to retry them.

Amid all of that, John Blair had committed himself to the Marble Hill and nuclear power debates to the point that it changed his life. "It was amazing," he says. "I almost lost all my friends, except the people who were just really my friends, because I became a bore. I became very consumed by nuclear energy. I was out to stop it."

His obsession, he adds, also caused him to pass up perhaps the biggest opportunity of his life. Because of receiving the Pulitzer, John, who had been raised in Bedford and North Vernon, was offered a job by the Gamma Liaison photo agency as its photographer in the South Pacific. He could have moved to Hawaii but chose to stay in Evansville. "I turned it down," he says. "I had just started the *OVE*, and I was committed to this. I was on a mission. I was really on a mission."

John and contributors to the *OVE* covered the gamut of environmental issues—toxic waste, water and air pollution, mining, environmental politics. But the publication's pages emphasized energy issues—nuclear, coal, synthetic fuels, nuclear fission—and reflected John's obsession with Marble Hill and nuclear power. In the thirty-six issues published between February 1979 and February 1982, *OVE* published nearly four dozen stories and editorials on those two subjects.

The first major story *OVE* carried on Marble Hill came in May 1979, when John reported in a copyrighted story that no disaster plan had been created for the plant. He stated that PSI in 1977 had filed a report saying it would "establish agreements with the appropriate local, state and federal agencies" for emergency preparedness. "Today, with less than three years until the plant is scheduled to open, PSI has signed 'no agreements' that they 'know of,' according to a company spokesman," John wrote. That same issue questioned whether nuclear power plants were being built to withstand earthquakes and noted that TMI was not the nation's first nuclear accident. It cited two other near-meltdowns at plants in Alabama and Michigan and other spills and problems at nuclear plants and storage sites.

In August 1979, John wrote about two major occurrences in the Marble Hill issue. One was the arrest of eighty-nine protesters during a second Paddlewheel Alliance occupation in June. His story focused on the one man who would go to trial, a fellow named Gardner Weber, the only protester to be arrested at both Paddlewheel occupations.

The other story was about an event that, in retrospect, would seem to have marked the beginning of the end for Marble Hill. The banner headline prophetically screamed "Marble Hill future in doubt." The story detailed defects in concrete work at the plant.

In June 1979, Marble Hill construction worker Charles Edward Cutshall provided Save the Valley with sworn statements that flaws in concrete work at Marble Hill had not been properly repaired. Shortly thereafter, other workers attested to the same facts. That led the NRC to twice order work stopped at the plant, and both Congress and the NRC launched investigations into what had happened. The congressional investigation came after the NRC had allowed contruction work to resume twelve days after the first shutdown, despite its inspectors' discovery of at least 500 defects in the concrete work, 170 of which had been improperly repaired.

John quoted Tom Datillo, an attorney and Save the Valley member who took Cutshall's statement, as saying that "thousands upon thousands" of the defects, called honeycombs, could exist at the plant. Honeycombs occur when concrete is poured over reinforcement bars and air becomes trapped in pockets. During hearings on the congressional investigation, Connecticut congressman Toby Moffett dubbed Marble Hill the "Three Mile Island of construction."

Though PSI maintained that "the concrete flaws at the plant are primarily cosmetic in nature and do not pose any threat to safety," the utility voluntarily halted safety-related work at Marble Hill indefinitely on August 8. Seven days later, the NRC made that voluntary move an order.

In late August, NRC inspectors placed the blame for the problems squarely on the shoulders of PSI management. Among other criticisms, the agency said that PSI had not hired enough inspectors, and that of the twenty-nine inspectors it did have, only four had experience with nuclear plants. "The NRC staff believes that in the recent past the management organization for the Marble Hill project has not functioned acceptably," the NRC said.

Meanwhile, the *OVE* kept hammering away at Marble Hill, PSI, and the NRC. John obtained a copy of a congressional committee report, which he quoted in a cover story in the September issue as saying that the NRC had "misled the American people as to the need for planning for nuclear accidents and lulled utilities and state and local officials into complacency." Other stories in that issue bore the headlines "PSI & Marble Hill beset with problems" and "PSI blames commies."

In his editorial, titled "Shut Marble Hill Down," John charged, "PSI's credibility is so riddled with deceit that it makes one wonder why they were able to build the plant as long as they have. . . . Unfortunately, PSI remains concerned only for their profitability and not for the health and safety of those who will face cancer and birth defects as a result of their shoddy construction."

It would be nineteen months before PSI would get the go-ahead to resume full construction. In March 1980, more than five hundred people jammed a public hearing in the Madison Junior High School to object to the restart that would be okayed twelve months later. In the interim, the NRC hired two independent consultants to review the concrete problems. The NRC approved construction before the consultants' reports were issued, leading John to question in a May 1981 *OVE* article, "Why, without the benefit of their own report, should they allow construction to resume?"

When the construction did resume, Datillo was quoted in the press as saying that while opponents were angry, they considered the nineteen-month shutdown at Marble Hill to have been their doing and therefore a victory. He also talked about changing tactics. By that time, PSI was estimating the cost at $3.4 billion. "Economics will probably tell a lot of tales," Datillo told the press. "The plant is already four years off schedule, and the estimate made by Fred Hauck, our engineer, is that it will cost more than $5 billion to build. They're going to try to squeeze it out of somebody. Our opinion is that Marble Hill is not a wise investment."

In August of 1981, the only other nuclear power plant proposed for Indiana, the Bailly plant in Porter County near the Indiana Dunes National Lakeshore, was scrapped for economic and design reasons. When the plant had been proposed in 1967, its price tag was $187 million. Legal battles and other delays—the project was put on hold in 1977—had forced the price to $1.8 billion when the Northern Indiana Public Service Company announced that it was canceling the plant.

Marble Hill faced the same fate. While there were other issues raised in the Marble Hill project—such as charges from a former worker in October 1983 that records had been falsified on "the patching of thousands of honeycomb defects"—much of the debate over Marble Hill after the construction restart focused on economics. By early 1983, PSI was estimating the price tag at $5.1 billion. In October, utility officials said that a computer analysis showed that the startup date might have to be moved from June 1986 to December, which would add even more.

As the construction costs continued to escalate, PSI kept arguing that even with the excess costs, the plant was still economically feasible. At a news conference in May 1983, the utility maintained its stance that Marble Hill power would be needed in the future and that it was still affordable. PSI senior vice-president Bill Shields: "With all the trials and tribulations we've been through, it's still the best choice. There will be rate shock at the time we go on line. There is no question that rates will go up. But it is still the best cost alternative for the consumers. . . . If you want to write this nation off as far as economic growth is concerned, then all bets are off. But if there is growth in the Gross National Product, and normal industrial growth, then this power is needed."

John, however, argues that the economics were never there for PSI and Marble Hill. "There was a fundamental flaw in PSI's thinking," he says. "PSI was going to add 25 percent to their capacity to generate electricity. But at the same time, in 1977, they were going to double their rate base. Now, that doesn't sound like a very good deal, on balance, and we exploited that. Then they were no longer doubling their rate base, they were quadrupling it. Well, there was no way that could ever be justified economically."

Opponents of Marble Hill repeatedly made those charges, comparing the effect the plant would have on the state to the Wabash Canal debacle of the 1830s. "I kept comparing it to the Wabash Canal, how the Wabash Canal caused Indiana to go broke, that Marble Hill, another unproven, very unreliable technology, was going to cause Indiana to go down the tubes."

In response to PSI's May 1983 press conference, John and Zeller called a press briefing of their own in Indianapolis to suggest a solution to PSI's increasingly desperate financial situation. "We called for PSI to go bankrupt," John says. "It was clear they were in trouble, big trouble. They couldn't borrow money. Their interest rates had gone from 10 percent to 15 percent, they had been taken down in their bond rating. They were in serious financial trouble for a plant that was only 20 percent complete."

Amid the financial dueling, Governor Robert Orr appointed a task force to study Marble Hill. It concluded that the project would cost $7.7 billion to complete, and recommended that it not be built and that ratepayers not be required to pay for it. In January 1984, after PSI had already spent $2.8 billion on the plant, PSI chairman Hugh Barker announced that the project was "financially and politically no longer feasible." The PSI board had canceled Marble Hill.

John never approached the *OVE* as a business; it was part of his cause, a labor of love, an instrument of his commitment to stopping Marble Hill and the proposed tri-state synfuel industry. By the time the last *OVE* rolled off the press in February 1982, the synfuels plants had been whipped, and Marble Hill, while still technically alive, had been irreparably injured. "Once Cutshall had come forward, it was clear that the epitaph had been written," John says. "We just exploited the hell out of that. And I'm not hesitant to use the word *exploit* at all. That's the name of the game. They made foolish statements, and we exploited them. In the process, we kept harping on the construction costs. Fred Hauck stayed on top of that. His final estimate was $14 billion, I think."

Through the years of the Marble Hill struggle, hundreds of people, if not thousands, took up the cause. But when Marble Hill went down, as John puts it, he called a handful of people to congratulate—Hauck, Gray, Cassidy, Zeller, and a woman named Mary Cash, who also had been active in Save the Valley. "I tried to think of everybody else that I thought deserved a pat on the back, and that was all I could come up with," he says. "Those were the people who stayed with it from 1973. I wasn't involved in it from 1973, and neither was Zeller. But from the time we got involved in '77, we were the ones who stayed with it through 1984."

While John on other occasions will say that there were maybe ten such people, his brazen reduction of the movement to such a tiny number is typical of the way he deals with the world. He speaks his mind with little regard for what others think about it. Acknowledging that fact, he says that such bluntness is premeditated and can be traced to early experiences he had in the working world. Early in his life, as happened at the University of Evansville, he had lost a couple of jobs for speaking out. "When I'd see an injustice, I'd open my mouth, and I'd get fired," he says. "It had almost gotten to be a routine."

John was mindful of that pattern when, after graduating from Indiana University with a bachelor's degree in economics, he took a job with an organization called the Greater Indianapolis Housing Development Corporation, working with inner-city people on housing problems. When Governor Otis Bowen in 1973 proposed his property tax relief program, which John calls "nothing but a windfall for business," he and the head of the Community Action Program in Indianapolis formed "a little taxpayers' union" to lobby for tax relief for renters. The day the hearings opened on the bill, there was a memo on everyone's desk in the company, a quasi-public corporation funded by the federal government, that said no member of the GIHDC was to participate in any lobbying activities without the prior consent of the board of directors. Figuring he didn't want to lose another job because of his mouth, John reluctantly went along.

"So the hearings came and went, and the bill was passed, and three days after the bill was signed, I was fired," he says. "I made a vow to myself that day; I was driving down Market Street toward the Capitol and made a vow to myself that if I ever had anything to say again, I was going to say it. It just didn't make any sense to keep my mouth shut because the same thing was going to happen to me no matter what. So I made that vow to myself, and I've lived up to it."

More than just John's insatiable desire to speak out causes him to attract attention. A stocky man with blond hair, a ruddy complexion, and a loud, booming voice, he has a commanding presence. While he was recounting his experiences in the Indiana environmental movement over coffee at the Evansville Ramada Inn, everyone within earshot cast an occasional curious glance toward the table to see the guy whose voice and views were ricocheting off the walls. A reporter for the *Evansville Courier* in February 1987 began a profile on John Blair: "You either love him or you hate him. You think he's a hero or a villain. He's either a champion of the common folk or a Don Quixote chasing environmental windmills. He's a big, brash man, always ready with an opinion. He's a tender daddy, awed by both the fragility and the strength of his two small children. He's John Blair—environmentalist, political activist, former political candidate."

He also is anything but humble. "I read things that people are talking about in the environmental movement today, and they are things that Tom and I were talking about in 1978," he says. "My ideas are so ahead of their time that the things I'm thinking today will not get a hearing until I die, until well past."

Ideas, according to Zeller, are what John Blair is all about. "He's always been interested in how public policy should be made, and on it being based on sound economic and free-enterprise principles," he says. "And when you look at Marble Hill, of course, you didn't have a free market situation, or that kind of outrageous expense would never have been proposed."

Zeller says that Blair's commitment to those ideals is one of the elements of his personality that set him apart from others. He's a proud American who believes that the United States can be a better place. Someone needs to pay attention to what government and industrial coalitions are doing. And John sees that as his role. "To Blair, democracy implies responsibility, that we're all responsible for getting involved in the issues, whether they involve a school board or the EPA. Somebody needs to pay attention. He believes that, and he's committed to that."

When John acts on that commitment, his style and knowledge of how things work in the public policy arena move to the forefront. He's implacable in his quest for information on issues. And he knows how to get his positions across. "John Blair is nothing if not dramatic," Zeller says. "If he cares about an issue, it's in the paper, it's on the front page, it's on TV, it's in the public consciousness. He has a knack for summing up a complicated situation in a sort of sound bite, and in a way that reflects what the crux of the issue is. He knows what journalists need. And pretty much when he's done, he knows what quotes are going to be in because he knows how it works."

John also has a passion for the fight. "If there were a written treatise on the warrior class, John Blair would have been the model for the thesis," says Tom Dustin. "He's a fighter from head to toe. He does not suffer fools gladly." John is at his best when the fight is "white hot" and he is manning the barricades himself, Dustin says. "If organized team effort is not his long suit, it must be said that he is almost as formidable single-handed."

And John refuses to defer to those in positions of power. He's neither affected nor impressed by titles. "He's equally willing to stand up and talk to a governor or a senator or the president of a big company and just talk to them like he would to you or me," Zeller says. But while his brazen approach may turn some people off, his positions are always backed up with solid facts and information. "He's always well based in the dramatic statements he makes," Zeller says. "From his research, he knows what he's talking about. He just couches his positions in the most dramatic terms possible. But I don't think he's ever gone over the edge in stating the situation."

John doesn't reserve his judgments solely for the enemy. At times he has turned his critical eye on his friends in the state's environmental movement. In November 1979 he wrote an editorial titled "Anti-Nuke Movement Needs Some Changes." Not only did he criticize movement leaders for being too distrustful of new people and for jealousy within the movement, he also called on environmentalists to clean up their appearance. "The public image of anti-nukes is very bad, causing most people to be skeptical of their appearance and style. . . . We may not like it but it's true that the straighter we look, the more influence we will have. This is not to say that everyone should look like Wall Street bankers, but effort should be made to look as presentable as possible any time we fight nuclear energy in public."

Such criticism cuts both ways for John Blair. "I've always been kind of an environmental gadfly," he says. "I figure I might as well because environmentalists are always criticizing me. I'm either too conservative or too radical."

John's radical side, and his propensity to create controversy, emerged when he served as president of the Hoosier Environmental Council in 1988. To his way of thinking, the movement is losing the war in Indiana. "Otherwise, we wouldn't be fiftieth in toxic pollution, fiftieth in air pollution, forty-ninth in water pollution, and all of that," he argues. Not understanding how the movement can be so passive in the face of those facts, he wrote an article for the HEC *Monitor* at the end of 1988 calling for more use of civil disobedience. The editor refused to run the article, saying that the president of the Hoosier Environmental Council couldn't be publicly advocating violating the law. What would that do to some of HEC's funding sources, John says she argued. "Well, basically, worrying about funding sources makes you a eunuch," John countered. "I guess that's why Valley Watch operates on twenty-five hundred dollars a year."

Civil disobedience is a philosophy that John Blair through the years has done more than just talk about. Aside from winning the Pulitzer, John is remembered by many as "the guy who stole the shovels," an act of civil disobedience that made him a media star in 1985. The issue was a proposed PCB recovery plant that Union Carbide was going to build in Henderson, Kentucky, just across the river from Evansville.

Not knowing that the plant was a done deal before they got involved, John and Valley Watch fought it tooth and nail. On the day that company and public officials were having a ground-breaking ceremony, John had other ideas. His original plan—to have some elderly women come to the ceremony and commandeer the shovels that were to be used—fell apart, so he decided to do it himself. Initially, he hoped to snatch the shovels quietly while the dignitaries were preoccupied with their ceremony. He was going to sneak the shovels to a truck driven by a friend and drive off with them. But security was too tight. So instead, John positioned himself next to a television reporter and cameraman and told them to keep their eyes on him. Just before the big moment, John swooped down on the shovels, scooped them up, and took off running until sheriff's deputies chased him down and tackled him a quarter-mile from the ceremony. During the chase, all eyes, including those behind the cameras, were on John Blair. The event created a minor media sensation throughout the entire Midwest.

"I'm not particularly a fan of passive civil disobedience like Paddlewheel did at Marble Hill when they climbed over the fence and got dragged off," he says, noting that he chose to cover the occupations as a journalist rather than as a participant. "My experience at Union Carbide says that the true form of civil disobedience that's going to excite the most response is active, nonviolent civil disobedience, not passive civil disobedience. Nonviolence is essential. But it can be active."

In fact, civil disobedience is one-third of an environmental-activism philosophy that John has been preaching for years. He calls it the "Three C's of the Environment."

First is confrontation. "Confrontation comes in a variety of forms, but you've got to confront the issue, whatever it is," he says. "You've got to define the issue very directly, know exactly what it is, and then go out in every venue you can and confront it." If environmentalists do not define an issue clearly and precisely and then confront it and the enemy, the opposition will define the issue for them and the battle will be lost before it is begun, John says.

Second is cooperation. "Once you confront the issue, you've got to hold out your hand and say, 'What can we do to resolve this issue?' and cooperate with them. You hope that they shake your hand and go forth in a very cooperative fashion to resolve the issue so that everybody gets out of it feeling proud of their position, and you achieve your goals."

If all of that fails, the only path left is civil disobedience, according to John's theory. "I guess that people don't perceive the problems as being acute enough," he says of the movement's unwillingness to sanction civil disobedience as a matter of course. "They may be chronic enough, but they're not acute enough for people to take that kind of action. Civil disobedience doesn't have to be a desperate act. It needs to be a well-thought-out and generally symbolic act."

⁕ ⁕ ⁕ ⁕

The hulking, partially complete concrete cooling towers, along with an assortment of outbuildings and other structures, remain standing at the Marble Hill Nuclear Generating Station site. They're just sitting there rusting, says John, who has been by the site a couple of times since the project was abandoned.

PSI was able to withstand the Marble Hill economic debacle, though its financial position was severely weakened by the excessive debt the utility piled up for the plant. While in truth there was no historical precedent for it, the demand for energy in Indiana and elsewhere did decrease in the years following the fall of nuclear energy, as John and other opponents had predicted. The Wabash Valley Power Association went into Chapter 11 bankruptcy after Marble Hill.

Under Indiana law, utilities are prohibited from charging customers for power plants that are in the process of being built. Ratepayers can be charged for construction costs only after a plant is producing energy. Attempts by PSI and sympathetic state legislators to change that law to allow costs of "construction work in progress" (CWIP) to be passed on to consumers were repeatedly defeated in the Indiana General Assembly. But John says even CWIP would not have saved Marble Hill. "They could not have pumped money into Marble Hill fast enough to ever finish it at the rate it was going," he says. "The cost of that construction was going up so rapidly that they couldn't spend it fast enough to ever finish it."

The same was, and is, true of nuclear power in general, John says. No matter what latter-day proponents of nuclear energy say, nuclear power is dead in the United States because the economics simply aren't there. "It's no accident that at the time we had the highest interest rates in our history, our modern history, 1979 and '80, was also the time that we had the biggest nuclear construction program that had ever been seen going on," he says. "There was like seventy plants, and they were skimming all the good capital off the top, all of it."

Interest rates had to climb because the utilities, convinced that they were going to make money hand over fist off nuclear power, were willing to pay 14 percent, according to John's analysis. But the utilities underestimated the depth of public opposition to nuclear power, not to mention the costs to build the plants as the public demanded stringent safety controls. Those costs and the opposition remain, making it highly unlikely that the country will turn to nukes again as an answer to its energy needs, John says.

But there is a scenario that worries him. While drinking in an Evansville bar one evening back around 1982, John struck up a conversation with an out-of-towner. Not knowing who John was, the guy told him that he worked for the Bechtel Corporation, a giant conglomerate that has, among other interests, built nuclear power plants all over the world. He said he was in Indiana for two reasons—to help the Indianapolis Power and Light Company build some pollution-control equipment at its Petersburg plant, and to scout a site for a nuclear power plant somewhere along the lower Wabash. The plan, the guy said, was to build a plant with private money and then lease it to a utility.

A reporter friend of John's checked out the man's story and hit a dead end. Bechtel said it had never heard of him, and as far as anyone knows, there were no plans for a nuke site in the area.

But that situation did point up a way that John says nuclear power could make a comeback in the United States. "Like I said, the capital markets will never support another nuclear power plant in the United States," he says. "Now if somebody like Bechtel comes in and wants to do it under the scenario that this guy painted for me ten years ago, it might get done. There might be other nukes built. But that's still an awfully risky venture. It would take somebody with an awful lot of money to risk to do that."

❧ ❧ ❧ ❧

HERB AND CHARLOTTE READ

Few environmentalists in the country have stayed with a single issue as long as Charlotte and Herb Read have with Indiana's Lake Michigan dunes. Herb's involvement dates to his youth, when he learned about the issue from his father, an early twentieth-century dunes preservationist. Herb's direct involvement began in 1952, when he joined the Save the Dunes Council, formed to establish a dunes national park and to fight off the plans of powerful political and economic interests to industrialize the entire Hoosier shoreline. Before the Indiana Dunes National Lakeshore was established, Herb and the council, with the help of Illinois senator Paul Douglas, carried the fight to the inner recesses of the Kennedy White House. Thanks to the work of the Save the Dunes Council and countless individuals, the 5,800-acre Indiana Dunes National Lakeshore was established in 1966.

Charlotte Read became active in dunes issues shortly after the park was established and has since kept up the struggle. As a leader in the Save the Dunes Council, Charlotte has been instrumental in resisting numerous development plans that would have despoiled the park, and in getting another 8,000-plus acres added to it. She was a founding member of the Hoosier Environmental Council and is active in several other environmental groups. Herb, sixty-nine, and Charlotte, sixty-six, live in the dunes, adjacent to the Indiana Dunes State Park, in a cabin where they raised five children.

Creating and Protecting a National Park

9 ❧ ❧ ❧ ❧ The roots of Herb Read's lifetime commitment to protecting the Indiana dunes can be traced to his days as a boy growing up in Chicago. His family lived on the southeast side of Chicago and would visit the dunes every week, sometimes for the weekend, sometimes just for the day, always hiking through and marveling at the unspoiled wonderland. His father was a member of the Prairie Club, an early twentieth-century conservation group that fought to preserve the dunes. "He was an artist and was always interested in the out of doors and hiking around," Herb says. "We just lived through the week in Chicago until we could come out here."

So when Indiana industrialists and politicians after World War II resurrected the idea of industrializing the state's Lake Michigan shoreline, Herb followed his family's tradition and got involved in efforts to protect the beloved sand hills that had so captured his imagination as a youth. In 1952, the same year he and Charlotte married, Herb joined the fledgling Save the Dunes Council, the latest incarnation of dunes preservation groups.

Herb's technical training as an architect and his knowledge of engineering would make him an invaluable contributor to the dunes struggle during the fourteen years between the council's formation and creation of the Indiana Dunes National Lakeshore.

His love affair with the dunes would keep him involved in these issues for the rest of his life.

While Charlotte also was active in the early days of the dunes struggle, she spent much of her time raising the couple's five children. She got more deeply involved as the park was being pieced together after it was authorized by Congress in 1966. She served as one of the first rangers at the park, a temporary, part-time position, and later became the Save the Dunes Council's first paid staffer. Since that time, Charlotte served as the council's executive director from 1974 to 1992 and has become one of the state's leading environmental voices.

Herb and Charlotte live in a cabin inside the boundaries of the Indiana Dunes National Lakeshore, from which they fought their four-decade-plus war for the dunes and raised their family. Together they are an awesome team, complementing each other perfectly. Herb is excitable. Charlotte is steady. As we sat around their kitchen table discussing their lives and the dunes, Charlotte frequently tried to rein Herb in as he would relate in minute detail aspects of the struggle to preserve and protect the dunes. As he munched on a bowl of granola and other whole grains, Herb would not be able to contain himself. "I have to tell this story," he excitedly said at one point, insisting on expanding the scope of the discussion. Charlotte patiently waited.

Perhaps as well as any other environmentalists in the state, Herb and Charlotte understand the most basic principles of environmental activism in Indiana. "The message is, the battle is never won," Herb says. "You have to keep watchdogging it. Generally speaking, political officeholders are oriented toward the developer. It is very, very, very rare that a political officeholder is not oriented toward further development—bigger and better and more. You use every angle that you can think of. You have to use all the tools."

The fight to protect the Indiana dunes unquestionably is the prototypical environmental battle in the state of Indiana. Taking on seemingly insurmountable odds—opponents such as giant steel companies and the entire Indiana legislative and congressional delegations in the days before the National Environmental Policy Act, open meetings laws, and the Freedom of Information Act—environmental activists such as the Reads won victories that today's best-prepared environmentalists would be proud of. Through sheer tenacity and force of intellect, the Reads and the Save the Dunes Council stymied their opponents' plans to industrialize twenty-five miles of Indiana shoreline along Lake Michigan and were able to preserve much of it as the state's only national park.

To be sure, the dunes struggle was anything but a complete victory. Two noxious steel plants and a deep-water port on Lake Michigan now sit where the finest examples of the Indiana dunes once towered above the lake. But rather than disappearing beneath bulldozers—as envisioned by Hoosier politicians from both sides of the aisle and northwestern Indiana economic development forces for nearly a half-century—14,000 acres of Indiana's dunes are now protected in perpetuity as state and national parkland. Within the national lakeshore boundaries lie giant sand dunes, swales, river forests, prairie lands, and bogs unlike any in the world. The park shelters more than fourteen hundred plant species—only four national parks contain more—and protects one species per ten acres, thirty-two times more diversity than its nearest counterpart.

In some respects, the fight for the dunes was also a prototype for the nation as a whole. In their attempts to prevent the area's natural wonders from becoming a footnote in natural history, Herb and others in the Save the Dunes Council developed tactics and strategies that had never been used before. They challenged the cost/benefit analysis put forth by the U.S. Army engineers. Today such challenges are routine and fundamental to public land-use battles everywhere.

"I think the council and George Anderson and Herb probably were the first people, long before it was popular, to take a Corps of Engineers study and challenge the figures and make them have to go back to the drawing board, twice," Charlotte says. "We still lost the battle, but it set the stage for citizens challenging the Corp of Engineers bureaucracy and the way they figured benefits and costs. As far as I know, that was the first attempt by citizens to do that."

The significance of the dunes issue was summed up in a September 23, 1963, editorial in the *New York Times:* "If the remarkable scenic, scientific and recreational resources of the Indiana Dunes are preserved for public use, millions of citizens in the crowded industrial areas of northern Illinois and Indiana will be particularly benefited and the whole nation will be grateful."

✦ ✦ ✦ ✦

By the time Herb and Charlotte sat down in 1992 to talk about their experiences in the Indiana environmental movement, the battle for Indiana's Lake Michigan shoreline and the dunes that frame it was more than two hundred years old and still ongoing. The first conflict over the region had its genesis in the Northwest Ordinance of 1787, which fixed the boundaries of Indiana, Ohio, and Illinois without giving Indiana any Lake Michigan shoreline. Jonathan Jennings, a delegate to Congress from the Indiana Territory, which was organized in 1800, argued for extensive boundary changes that would have given the state lengthy shoreline in what is now Michigan. Facing staunch opposition from Michigan Territory delegates, Jennings compromised. When the state of Indiana was organized in 1816, it included eleven hundred acres and forty-five miles of shoreline that had been Michigan's.

Jennings's vision proved to be farsighted given the attitudes about the sandy, swampy topography he had argued over. In 1821, the state sent John Tipton north from the state capital at Corydon to survey the lake area. His assessment: "Covering the shore are small pine and cedar trees very few large enough for building or other use. Most of the way, the margin of the lake is lined with small hills of white sand rising five to ten feet above the country in back of them. . . . It is my opinion the hills are formed by the sand beating out of the Lake by the waves when it becomes dry. The hard wind which prevails here from the north drives it into those heaps. Immediately behind those hills the country falls off into ponds and marshes that never can admit of settlement nor never will be of much service to our state."

Tipton's analysis of the dunes displayed a naivete about dunes ecology. The five-to-ten-foot-high hills are what are called "foredunes." The forested hills inland from the lake are also dunes. The high dunes, which reach heights of two hundred feet and more, are covered with a layer of soil that supports full-grown trees.

Indeed, the unforgiving landscape of the dunes area led early settlers to avoid northwest Indiana altogether. Instead they followed the Erie Canal, completed in 1825, to the Great Lakes and then on to northern Ohio, southern Michigan, and later Illinois and Wisconsin. In 1850, two decades after Chicago's population had reached about 70,000, Lake and Porter counties had scant populations of 3,991 and 5,234 respectively. In that same year, Congress ceded swamplands to host states under the provision that proceeds from the land sales would go to reclamation. In

Indiana, the value of dune country land skyrocketed. In 1852 it had been $1.25 per acre. By 1854, it was $42.95.

The seeds of the conservation–industrial development clash were sown in the latter half of the nineteenth century, when two distinct views of the region's value developed.

In 1872 John Coulter, former Indiana University president and chairman of the University of Chicago's botany department, conducted the first known scientific exploration of the dunes. Twenty-seven years later, his successor in the department, Henry Cowles, began what would become a lifelong practice of bringing classes to the dunes for field observations. Cowles would later become known as the father of the study of ecology; the dunes would become known as the birthplace of the science of ecology.

Countering the nascent scientific interest in the dunes were visions of industrial conquest by those who saw dollar signs rather than natural treasures on the shoreline. In 1889, Standard Oil decided to build a lakeshore refinery in Whiting, just across the state line from Chicago. In 1892, iron ore was discovered in Minnesota's Mesabi range, opening the gate to steel production in the western Great Lakes region.

The early twentieth century saw both of those forces intensify their efforts.

In 1901, more than two hundred steel companies merged to form U.S. Steel, which four years later began secretly developing plans for a steel mill at the southern tip of Lake Michigan. A year later, land deals were completed, construction began on the company's Gary Works, and the town of Gary was created. In the process, the sand dunes along that stretch of lakeshore were leveled and lost forever. In 1908, a Chicagoan named Randall W. Burns, who owned twelve hundred acres of Gary marshland, proposed rechanneling the Little Calumet River to prevent flooding of Gary in the spring. Eighteen years later, an eight-and-a-half-mile channel known as Burns Ditch was cut, more than a mile of it through the high dunes area in western Porter County.

Coincident with the intensifying industrial interest in the Indiana lakeshore was an ever-growing appreciation of the region's unique natural characteristics by conservation-minded Chicagoans. In 1909, the city's Playground Association, forerunner of the Prairie Club, began its "Saturday Afternoon Walks," the first organized group exploration of the dunes. By 1913 the group had established a camp at Tremont with a permanent beach house, rustic cabins, and tenting platforms. A year later, the group formed the Conservation Council of Chicago, a coalition of conservation groups with a goal of preserving the twenty-five-mile stretch of dunes between Gary and Michigan City.

Among those who were active in the early days were Jens Jensen, a Danish immigrant who became Chicago's parks superintendent and argued for rings of park and forest preserves to surround the city; Stephen Mather, who would become head of the nation's fledgling national park system; and Gary's Bess Sheehan, who, as leader of the State Federated Woman's Club's Dunes Park Committee, would lead the early conservation fight and earn the title "Lady of the Dunes."

A number of events occurred in 1916, the year of the state's centennial celebration and the year that Sheehan assumed leadership of the dunes park committee, that gave rise to hope for those seeking to save the dunes. Disenchanted with the industrialization of Gary, former Hammond mayor and attorney A. F. Knotts, who had chosen the Gary Works site for U.S. Steel in 1905, helped form the National Dunes Park Association, formalizing a base of support in Indiana for a park. Congress passed National Park Service Bureau legislation that had been promoted by Mather. Democrat Tom Taggart, a supporter of a dunes national park, was appointed to the U.S. Senate and introduced legislation directing the federal government to purchase the dunes. On October 30 a public hearing was held on the proposed Sand Dunes National Park. Two months later, the Park Service recommended that a twenty-five-mile-long, one-mile-deep park be established between Gary and Michigan City.

1917, however, would be as disappointing for dune preservationists as 1916 had been encouraging. Taggart lost his bid for a full term in the Senate, and Mather left the Park Service. The Sand Dunes National Park proposal never got a congressional hearing. The politics simply weren't there, a situation predicted in industrial supporter A. J. Bowser's Chesterton *Tribune:* "With the present line-up of Congress, it seems improbable that Mr. Mather's scheme of planning national parks all over these United States will have a smooth sailing. Mr. Taggart will be a private citizen on December 4 and his resolution will be without a father."

Undeterred, dunes supporters on Memorial Day 1917 turned out in record numbers for "the Great Pageant" at Waverly Beach.

More than forty thousand people weathered early rains and late-afternoon heat over the two-day event to lend their support to dunes preservation. More than five hundred actors and musicians put on a pageant unlike any ever seen in the area. Herb's father was on the "Properties and Costumes" committee. Uniformed Campfire Girls solicited donations for the National Dunes Park Association. But despite the pageant's unprecedented success in raising awareness of the issue, no politician stepped forward to take up where Taggart had left off.

Dunes supporters by 1919 had reluctantly come to accept that the political will for a national park not only wasn't there, it would not be forthcoming. Another event that year would likewise contribute to the sense that the Sand Dunes National Park was a lost cause. Inland Steel purchased thirteen hundred acres of land that had been proposed for the park, including one mile of lakeshore in western Porter County that abutted Lake County.

Many dunes supporters began setting their sights on a state park instead. That route was further paved in September when Bowser surprised everyone at a meeting of the National Dunes Park Association by saying that industrial boosters would support a state park. The proposal was for an 8,000-acre park with an eight-mile shoreline. A few months later, the NDPA reluctantly endorsed the idea.

On March 6, 1923, Indiana governor Warren T. McCray signed legislation authorizing creation of the Indiana Dunes State Park. The original proposal was pared down, however, and four years later, enough land had been purchased that a 2,182-acre state park was created on the Lake Michigan shoreline just north of Chesterton.

Content with their accomplishment, conservationists, for all practical purposes, took a thirty-year hiatus from their dunes-preservation activities. They wouldn't reorganize again until after World War II.

Those who eyed the shoreline in Porter County as a future home for industrialization did not slow their march following the state park's creation. They knew what they wanted—a deep-water port that would bring economic development to the region. And they knew where they wanted it. In 1928, Midwest Steel purchased 750 acres of duneland that straddled the mouth of the

Burns Ditch at Lake Michigan. Both public and private proponents agreed that the port had to be public. The steel companies
did not want to pay for it. And economic development boosters
saw a public port as a means to promote growth in the entire
area. In addition, a public port would allow the government to
take land for it by eminent domain.

Industrial proponents howled in 1928 when a developer named
Nelson Reck petitioned the War Department for federal approval of
a "pleasure yacht harbor" where the ditch met the lake. "As this
inlet called the Burns Ditch is the only harbor available in Porter
County, Indiana, for commercial purposes . . . Porter County will be
harmed tremendously and her industrial development in this natural strategic location will be forever foreclosed" if the yacht harbor
were allowed, Valparaiso Chamber of Commerce director John
Griffin wrote to the army engineers. He and other port proponents
convinced Indiana congressman William R. Wood to get the federal
government to initiate a commercial harbor survey. In December
1931, the army engineers rejected a port at Burns Ditch without
even holding a hearing. Their position was that the port would be
surrounded by Midwest Steel and therefore be inaccessible to the
public. The yacht harbor never got off the drawing board.

By 1935, several events had occurred to encourage port proponents. The first of seven pro-port governors had been elected in
1932; Republican Charlie Halleck, who would ascend to the position of Speaker of the House and carry the pro-industry and anti-
park banner for more than thirty years, had been elected to the
Second District House seat; and four years of negotiations with
Midwest Steel had produced a package of promises that enhanced
the odds that the army engineers would reverse their 1931 position.

In 1935, Halleck got the House Committee on Rivers and Harbors to pass a resolution requesting that the 1931 army engineers
report be re-evaluated. But citing economic conditions, particularly the below-capacity condition of existing steel mills, the engineers again rejected the port. The state appealed, and lost.

In the meantime, the National Park Service in 1934 had initiated a two-year study of seashores along the Atlantic and Gulf of
Mexico shorelines. In 1937, the Cape Hatteras National Seashore
off the North Carolina coast was created, the nation's first.

By 1938, port proponents' stock had plummeted again. The
army engineers once again refused to survey the lakeshore for a
port. And Midwest Steel refused to renew its 1935 pledges, in part

because it had spent $27 million in Detroit that had been planned for Indiana.

In 1939, port supporters, as conservationists had more than a decade before, accepted that the federal government was not going to be their savior. And, also as their opponents had done, they turned to the state of Indiana. In that year George Nelson, secretary of the Valparaiso Chamber of Commerce, lobbied the legislature for $1 million for the Burns Ditch Harbor. Even though Nelson walked away with only a $50,000 appropriation, he had gotten the first state money dedicated to the project. And he and state senator John Van Ness, a former Valparaiso chamber director, got the state to create a Board of Harbors and Terminals, which would aid in developing a case for the Burns Ditch Harbor.

The port effort lay dormant between that time and the end of World War II. A country preoccupied with war paid little attention to a port in northwestern Indiana. But in 1949, port proponents again approached the army engineers, this time with different results. A public hearing held in Gary on July 19 produced a report calling for a survey of the Lake Michigan shoreline.

Alarmed, conservationists reorganized as a group called the Indiana Dunes Preservation Council. After an initial flurry of activity, the council turned out to be rather ineffective. Among the true conservationists in the group was Dr. Myron Reuben Strong, who had long been active in the dunes effort. Worried about the faltering preservation effort, Strong on February 24, 1952, wrote to an Ogden Dunes woman named Dorothy Buell: "I wish to discuss with you the problem of leadership for our effort to save the dunes between Ogden Dunes and Dune Acres. . . . We lack aggressive leadership. We need a more active campaign than we've seen so far. . . . It is my judgment that we need someone who will do what Mrs. Sheehan did in the promotion of the Indiana Dunes State Park, and I think you may be the person to do this."

In June 1952, Dorothy Buell formed the Save the Dunes Council.

Mrs. Buell initially fashioned the Save the Dunes Council after the model established by Sheehan. It was an all-women's organization, focusing exclusively on creation of a park. As time passed, however, men came to join and to play increasingly important roles. Among them was Herb, whose technical training as an architect and engineer prepared him for a crucial role. With the men's participation, the council's mission expanded to stopping the port, as well as creating a park. The proposed port location was in the heart of the best of the remaining dunes.

Herb says that industrial proponents were interested in more than just the Porter County shoreline. They wanted to create what they called Indiana's "industrial crescent," an industrial zone covering the entire lakeshore from Gary to Michigan City. "They planned to get rid of the state park, get rid of the homes along there," he says. "At that time they thought industry was going to grow forever."

Council members' initial strategy was to prevent that by buying up the dunes and shoreline with privately donated funds. In 1953 they learned that what was thought to be Cowles Bog, the site of Cowles's early scientific studies, was going to be put on the auction block at a tax sale. The council bought it.

But, Herb says, such an approach displayed a political naiveté that would have been crushed by the powerful interests the council was facing. There obviously wasn't enough money to win with that strategy. Then they went to state officials and tried to convince them to enlarge the west end of the state park to stave off the industrial expansion. But there they were seeking aid from the enemy. It didn't matter whether the politicians they approached were Democrats or Republicans, state or federal or local, they all favored industrializing the lakeshore.

In 1954, Indiana governor George Craig proposed that the state borrow $3.5 million to purchase 1,500 acres of Porter County shoreline for harbor development. That same year, Congress appropriated $4,000 for the survey called for in the 1949 army engineers' report, though the study would be delayed because of the Korean War. The legislature did not approve Craig's request, but it did approve a feasibility study that reported positively on the port proposal.

It would have been easy, perhaps even understandable, if members of the Save the Dunes Council had given up. But they didn't. They went over the politicians' heads and took their case to the people. They started petition drives, they took photographs of the area to show its natural splendor, they sang the praises of the Indiana dunes to any group or organization that would listen. They enlisted volunteers to produce a movie about the area. "We'd take this film and go out four or five or six nights a week showing it to groups and give little talks, everything from large groups to little women's sewing circles," Herb says. "And over the years, that built public awareness where the awareness hadn't been before."

By 1956, the Save the Dunes Council had 1,000 members and a goal of raising $1 million. By 1958, it had petitions supporting the park with more than a half-million signatures.

The council members also educated themselves. "We said, first of all, we have to know everything we can about the Indiana dunes—geological things, natural areas—become totally familiar with the subject, educate ourselves while we educate the public. That's step number one," Herb says. "Step number two was know our enemy. Know what our enemy was saying, and investigate whether the enemy was telling the truth, which in this case they weren't."

To accomplish the second part of the strategy, the council needed to understand the incredibly complex engineering and economic issues involved in the port-park battle. Herb and others, most notably an economist/engineer named George Anderson, convinced Mrs. Buell to let them form an engineering committee to work on that angle. Time and again that committee would make the difference between success and failure.

But the council still lacked the political champion needed to carry on the fight. And while they were gaining widespread public support, they were losing the political battle. In 1957, the Indiana legislature passed a bill permitting the state to build a port without federal participation and approved spending $2 million on it, even though the money wouldn't actually be made available until the mid-1960s.

In the spring of that year, a frustrated Dorothy Buell called Emily Taft Douglas, wife of Democratic senator Paul Douglas from Illinois. She asked if Douglas could be of help in the fight for the dunes, a request that would forever alter the nature of the struggle.

In May 1958, Douglas introduced federal legislation to establish a 4,000-acre national park in the Indiana dunes, the first of several park bills he would sponsor. The park would have included three and a half miles of Porter County shoreline, including the Central Dunes, the most spectacular on the lakeshore located between Ogden Dunes and Dune Acres. The Central Dunes were owned by the Midwest and Bethlehem steel companies and the Northern Indiana Public Service Company (NIPSCO).

From that moment on, Paul Douglas orchestrated the fight for the dunes in the halls of Congress.

🙦 🙦 🙦 🙦

Douglas's entry into the dunes fray was followed by four years of jockeying by each side, with neither able to gain the upper hand. But industry did make tremendous strides in some important battles.

In 1959, Bethlehem Steel and NIPSCO swapped some land in the Central Dunes area so that the utility could construct a power plant to supply electricity to the planned steel mill. Bethlehem in that same year assisted in the creation of the city of Portage, which not surprisingly adopted a pro-industry zoning stance.

Midwest Steel built a $100 million plant on its Porter County property and began shipping steel from it in March 1961. In April, Bethlehem Steel contracted with Northwestern University to sell it sand from its Central Dunes holdings for a landfill. Leveling of the dunes for the project began in April 1962, destroying the finest examples of Indiana dunes for eternity.

The state in May held hearings to determine where the best site would be for a Porter County port, which it would quickly conclude was the dunes site between Bethlehem and Midwest Steel.

Meanwhile, Douglas in 1961 had proposed a 9,000-acre park, which included 2,054 acres in the Central Dunes. In July, he and the Save the Dunes Council conducted a highly public tour of the dunes for high-ranking federal officials, including Interior Secretary Stewart Udall, National Park Service Director Conrad Wirth, and Senator Alan Bible, whose subcommittee would hold hearings on Douglas's park bills.

All to no avail. In February 1962, the army engineers agreed with the state, issuing a report saying that the Burns Harbor site in the dunes was the best available for a port. In July, Indiana governor Matthew Welsh met with President Kennedy to stress the importance of a port to Indiana's economy. By that time, the state had acquired all but 100 acres of the 440 needed for a port. In August the federal Budget Bureau met with the army engineers to work out a proposal for Congress.

In response to all of that, Herb and the council decided to challenge the army engineers' cost-benefit analysis, which had to justify using public funds to finance building a port. Their initial review, completed in August 1962, found that the army engineers had used numerous unjustified assumptions, which Herb says were "totally unrealistic and totally wrong." Douglas then went to President Kennedy and convinced him to have the U.S. Budget

Bureau investigate the discrepancies between the council's and corps' analyses. There followed a series of meetings in Washington at which Herb and George Anderson faced off with corps officials over their differences. "We'd lay out our figures, and they'd lay out their figures, and we managed to checkmate them," Herb says. The Budget Bureau on two occasions concluded that the council's analysis was right.

In the interim, the industrialization of the Indiana dunes was on hold because of the stalemate. "They stopped the park, but we stopped the port," Charlotte says. "So it came down to the Kennedy administration worked out a compromise, which gave Indiana some of the best of the dunes, a small industrial crescent, and the prospect for a large national park."

That compromise came about as the result of a frantic last-minute bit of lobbying by Douglas. In early October 1962, a wire-service reporter called a Douglas aide, telling him that he had seen a Budget Bureau authorization for a public works bill that included the Burns Harbor site. The authorization had been signed by President Kennedy, the reporter said, explaining that he had read it upside down on a bureau official's desk. The aide told Douglas, who immediately had his secretary call the White House to tell Kennedy that he was on his way. While walking through the Rose Garden with the young president, Douglas convinced him that the army engineers' cost-benefit analysis contained errors.

"A day or two later I got a call from Douglas that there was a meeting in Washington tomorrow," Herb says. "'Be here and be prepared to explain the Corps of Engineers' mistakes,' he said. 'By the way, what are they?' I said. 'I don't know. We haven't found them yet. But we'll find them.'" Herb and George Anderson then boarded an overnight train for Washington and spent the entire trip poring over the army engineers' reports. "By the time we got there, we had identified their mistakes. The Corps of Engineers had been double- and triple-counting benefits between districts. The Louisville district was counting the same benefits as the Chicago district for Burns Harbor."

Herb, Anderson, and Douglas spent the next day making their case at meetings with army officials and representatives from the White House staff. "We understand that after that meeting somebody said, 'Let's settle this damn thing. Let's come up with some kind of compromise,'" Charlotte says. To that point, only Indiana senator Vance Hartke had ever proposed a compromise, a 1961 bill that called for a port and a 6,000-acre park that excluded the

Central Dunes. Halleck and the port supporters refused to even discuss a compromise.

The Budget Bureau then rejected the army engineers' report again, and in August 1963 approved a proposal that allowed a port and an 11,700-acre national park. Two more years of jockeying over funding and other details followed before Congress passed a port bill on October 27, 1965. The park bill passed a year later, on October 14.

-✹- -✹- -✹- -✹-

Passage of the long-awaited Indiana Dunes National Lakeshore Bill, however, was a bittersweet victory for the Reads and other dunes supporters. By the time House Democrats outmaneuvered Halleck on the final vote—Halleck vehemently opposed any national park in the dunes until the very end—the park bill was a mere ghost of what had been called for in the compromise of 1963. "The people who had sworn allegiance to the compromise, our opponents, said, 'Compromise? What compromise?'" Herb says. "The park bill then got chopped down to 8,000 acres, including the state park. Actually, 5,800 acres of national lakeshore, as it passed in 1966. And it almost didn't get passed."

At that time, Herb says, Save the Dunes Council members felt that they could disband after having accomplished their goals, even if they had lost ground in the end. They had dramatically cut back the area to be industrialized and had guaranteed that part of the Indiana dunes would be preserved. But, as Charlotte says, council members still had a lot to learn. "We learned about the two-step process. You get authorization to do something. Then you have to get the money. And there was no money to buy it."

Because Herb simply couldn't continue devoting so much time to the day-to-day fights for the park, and their four boys and one girl had been raised, Charlotte became more active at that point. At first she testified before appropriations committees seeking money to get the park established. But she soon learned that each little victory is followed by another fight. "You find that in order to accomplish your goal, your activities spread out like the spokes on a wheel. Otherwise, what you thought you had done isn't going to get done because of all these other forces—intrusion, pollution, failure of the managing agency. You get into a whole big environmental activity."

The spokes of the Reads' wheels have indeed continued to radiate outward since the couple first got involved in the duel for the dunes forty years ago. Along the way they have kept up the fight to add new areas to the park and to protect the integrity of what they already had achieved. The park, following the 1990 congressional session, had reached 14,000 acres. Herb and Charlotte say there are probably another 2,000 to 3,000 acres that should be included to create the best national park there can be in northern Indiana.

They also have had to fight some unexpected battles. At one point in the 1960s, they had to resist plans by NIPSCO to build the Bailly nuclear power plant adjacent to the national park. In the early 1980s, the State Recreation Development Commission proposed a plan to develop a conference center/hotel/parking garage complex on the western third of the state park. In the late 1980s, a Gary developer proposed building private condominiums and an 18,000-seat lakefront arena for rock concerts on park duneland. And in 1990 NIPSCO wanted to develop a project called Crescent Dunes Estates—two hundred townhouses, a restaurant, and an industrial area—on land within the authorized park boundaries but still owned by the utility. And those are just a few of the "great ideas" that developers and government officials have come up with that the Save the Dunes Council has had to resist, Herb says.

Some battles, Charlotte adds, had to be waged against the very agency entrusted with protecting the park—the National Park Service. At one point the agency had plans to allow a 1,000-car marshaling yard for the South Shore Railroad tracks inside the park boundaries. On other occasions, park officials had come up with plans for developments reminiscent of "miniature Disneylands"—pools, tennis courts, artificial dunes, parking lots. "You never know when you're going to have to refight the battles that you've already won, in addition to having to fight new battles that you sometimes generate and sometimes respond to," Charlotte says.

❀ ❀ ❀ ❀

Both Herb and Charlotte have been involved in numerous environmental groups and issues. In the late 1950s, Herb founded the Porter County chapter of the Izaak Walton League, one of the region's strongest voices for environmental protection. Charlotte was a co-founder of the Hoosier Environmental Council. Together they have garnered numerous joint awards for their environmental activities, including the 1990 Lifetime Achievement Award from the Hoosier Environmental Council, the 1991 Gold Cup Award from the Hoosier Sierra Club, and two industry-sponsored awards.

Mary Kay Rothert, who was on the founding board of the Hoosier Environmental Council along with Charlotte, says that Charlotte played a moderating role during discussions on the council's role. "She would sit there and always be practical. People would say, 'Oh, yes, we'll do this and we'll do that,' and, 'Let's have an organization that does X, Y, and Z.' Charlotte was always the one who would say, "Look, let's keep it realistic.' She would ask questions that would make you realize that you were sort of over the cliff in terms of what you were imagining."

Long-time colleague Bill Hayden calls Herb a character who's done some "really incredible things" that he says are probably best left unpublished. All he will say is that they involved some of Herb's tactics in resisting dunes development. As for Charlotte, he calls her "contrary." If the governor proposes one thing, Charlotte is against it. If he proposes the opposite, Charlotte's against it. "Charlotte is more radical than most of us," Hayden says. "They're not going to satisfy Charlotte. And she's not dumb. She didn't grow up in Indiana. She grew up in Chicago. She doesn't have a whole lot of admiration for Indiana politicians."

Tom Dustin worked with the Reads in the early days of the Save the Dunes Council and knows them as well as anyone in the state. "I have never known more fearless people," he says. "Resolute determination, exceptional expertise, the ability to endure combat and to strike two blows for every one received are among their characteristics. If I had to go to war in any major environmental battle, the two people I would want back to back over armies of other worthies would be Herb and Charlotte Read. I really can't think of any downsides where the Reads are concerned."

✢ ✢ ✢ ✢

In their forty-plus years fighting for the environment, Herb and Charlotte Read have earned the highest praise bestowed upon them by their colleagues. They have encountered and overcome just about every issue and obstacle that environmentalists can face. And they cite several strategies that they say should be followed in public lands issues: know the politics of the issue at hand and become thoroughly familiar with it and the opposition; always tell the truth and have the facts nailed down; and work with other groups, even if there's not always agreement on where they stand on other issues.

Understanding the issue and opposition is critical because of the built-in political bias against environmentalists and in favor of development. Politicians are always looking for ways to deny those fighting for the public interest. And they often are willing to go to extreme lengths to do so, as Herb and George Anderson learned in the dunes struggle. In their reviews, they uncovered more than just incorrect assumptions and miscalculations on the part of the Army Engineers. They uncovered outright deceit and fraud on the part of state officials.

The Indiana Port Commission and the Corps of Engineers, for example, were supposed to study the entire shoreline to come up with the best location for a deep-water port. At a public hearing, the council and others provided the commission with reams of information about the shoreline. But the commission took only ten days to announce its decision. "They couldn't have even read the materials," Herb says. "We didn't know it at the time, but they had this secret agreement with the steel companies which pinpointed the site right there." In 1957, Bethlehem Steel had given the state a purchase option for 260 acres of its Burns Harbor property, with the stipulation that it would revert back to the company if port construction had not begun by 1968. And in 1960, Bethlehem and Midwest secretly agreed to pay the state $4.5 million for part of the port's construction.

Sometimes such deceit isn't even hidden or disguised. During the fight over the nuclear power plant, NIPSCO engineers submitted maps to the Nuclear Regulatory Commission board that misrepresented the area to show that the plant would not pose a threat to the region's population. "They moved the boundary of Gary seven miles to the west," Herb says. "They didn't show the city of Portage at all. And there was five or six other towns not on the maps, because if they had been they would have shown that the proposed plant site was not out in the boonies." The maps also showed the national park boundary to be five miles away, when in fact it abutted the NIPSCO land and was eight hundred feet from the reactor. At one point Herb photographed a ten-story apartment building located at a spot the NIPSCO maps said was covered with forest and undeveloped. "The NRC board concluded that since NIPSCO and the NRC had mapmakers, the maps must be right and the photo wrong."

⊛ ⊛ ⊛ ⊛

To counter the bias and the tactics of the enemy, the Reads say environmentalists must always have their facts down pat and never get caught telling lies or exaggerating the truth. The opposition may get away with such blatant deceit. Environmentalists cannot. "The only thing we have to sell is our credibility and accuracy," Herb says. "We should never exaggerate our case. We should make sure everything we say is absolutely correct. You catch them in a lie, they go on to the next lie. If we say something that's incorrect, they'll throw it back at us for years and years and years."

Another major threat to environmentalists' chances for success is dissension from within, a tendency for their efforts to be compromised by infighting. The Save the Dunes Council has been able to avoid that pitfall, the Reads say, by keeping its focus on the bigger picture. "We've never had a lot of infighting," Charlotte says. "There have been people who have been unhappy, no doubt about it. But on the whole, we have expanded the core, and the group has come together and continued to stay together. We've been able to stick together and work together."

Environmental activists have to understand that their numbers are so small and their fights so important that they can't waste their resources bickering with each other, whether it is inside a specific group or within the movement as a whole. They have to support each other in order to survive as a movement. Charlotte cites the cooperation between dunes proponents and those fighting for the Hoosier National Forest in southern Indiana. "It certainly wasn't our primary effort. But we circulated petitions, and we wrote letters a couple of times on the Hoosier National Forest. And in reciprocity, we have gotten help on the dunes. This last dunes expansion bill involved pressure on Senator Coats from all over the state, or he wouldn't have changed his mind and supported it."

Herb says environmentalists must not compete with each other in the political arena. "I have seen this happen in a few cases where the pie is only so big, and each one is trying to get its pet project approved from that piece of the pie. Take the position that 'Yes, we think that our project should be the one that is approved.

But we fully support our friends on their project.' That's a number one axiom for me."

Nor should groups be judgmental about other groups. There is a tendency among some of the newer environmental groups to demand purity in their allies. "I look at the total picture," Herb says. "Is the total picture beneficial to the environment? If it is, I go along with it. Nobody's 100 percent pure."

Perhaps the biggest obstacle, which fortunately many environmentalists aren't aware of when they first become active, is the depth of commitment needed to be truly successful. "I think political astuteness is not what gets you into it in the first place," Charlotte says. "It's something you learn somewhere down the line. I think it has to be a fools-rush-in type of thing. If you knew what you were getting into, you'd never do it. If you were told, 'You've got something you want to save, figure on forty to fifty years,' you'd say, 'Forget it, I'm not interested.' You get hooked on the little victories, and the little defeats, and then pretty soon you find, at least in our case, that it becomes the central part of your life. There's no finite point when you can say, 'It's over, I can rest.' Eternal vigilance is the price of preserving your good idea. I mean, it's just so clear."

❧ ❧ ❧ ❧

STEVEN HIGGS has been writing about the Indiana environment for more than a decade. A public affairs reporter for the Bloomington *Herald Times*, he has won numerous awards for his work from the Associated Press Managing Editors Association, the Society of Professional Journalists, the Indiana Judges Association, and the Indiana Society for Healthcare Public Relations and Marketing. He was named the 1994 Journalist of the Year by the Hoosier Environmental Council. His work has appeared in the *Indianapolis Star* and in *Traces of Indiana and Midwestern History*. He has been a guest lecturer at the Indiana University School of Journalism since 1987.